Modern Jewish Cooking
with Style

Modern Jewish Cooking with Style

*Innovative and Contemporary
Kosher Recipes for all Occasions*

Denise Phillips

Robson Books

In loving memory of my wonderful husband
Michael Phillips, who inspired and
encouraged me to write this book.

To my fabulous children, Abbie, Samantha and
Nicholas, for their patience, continuous support and love.

First published in Great Britain in 2000 by Robson Books,
10 Blenheim Court, Brewery Road, London N7 9NT

A member of the Chrysalis Group plc

Copyright © 2000 Denise Phillips
Photographs © 2000 David Murray
Line drawings by Carole Vincer
Method illustrations by Roger Leboff

British Library Cataloguing in Publication Data
A catalogue record for this title is available from the British Library

ISBN 1 86105 317 7

Photographs styled by Clare Carter
Designed by Katrina ffiske

Printed in Spain

Contents

Acknowledgements

I would like to thank Simone Leboff, who has been a friend and partner for many years, for her help putting this book on disc and for her hours of typing, advice, comments and assistance at cookery school. I would also like to thank another close friend, Marsha Schultz who helped to edit the recipes and copy. Between them both, I have had someone to call on morning, noon and night about an idea or experiment. Their understanding husbands deserve a worthy mention, Roger and Martin respectively, because they have been there to provide child care whilst their wives have been working with me.

No book is a success without marketing and financial input and a big thank you to my cherished friends, Michael and Susan Hutter for their time and effort spent with me working on these areas.

I am very proud of my good friend, Lynne Misner for writing a computer programme especially for me and greatly appreciate all her help with the book. Thank you to Sue Levy for organising a synagogue data base which will be widely used for many years to come.

Many thanks go to Robson Books and their editing team and David Murray and Jules Selmes for the food photography.

A special thanks to Ozzie Jung for the photographs he took in his free time for the launch of the book and the Jewish Press.

I have an extremely supportive family - parents, in-laws, and sisters. There is no doubt that I could not have achieved this book without their love, encouragement and help.

I have received much comfort and spiritual support from Rabbi Brawer for which I am eternally grateful. A thank you to Rebbetzin Dina Brawer whose contributions on Kashrut have been invaluable.

Eric Treuville, of Books for Cooks believed from day one that I had a great idea. He also introduced me to the right people in the publishing world for which I am very grateful.

Thank you to Neil Isaacson, of Amazing Grapes for his time and advice on Kosher wine

Lastly, I would like to thank the following people who took part in the cookery trials for their comments and suggestions which were very helpful. I hope you enjoyed my experimental dishes: Lynne Misner; Helen mcGuigan; Sue Morgan; Marsha Schultz; Sharon Phil-lips; Liz Maykels; Rica Green; Freda Skovron; Nicki Wilkinson; Ellie Olmer; Jill Green; Susan and Michael Hutter; Louise St Hill; Sharman Berwald; Harriet Sacks; Simone Leboff; Audrey Kostick; Helly Cramer; Rebbetzin Dina Brawer; Mandy Guest; Aviva Wilford; Gilly Freed; Janet Brand; Michael Davidson; Debbie Sands; Laura Lehmann; Carolyn Joels; Linda Abrahams; Gail Weinstein; Joy Gregan; Maryse and Julian Shields; Mandy Hircombe; Sarah Starr; David Murray; Caroline and Michael Weber.

Introduction

It was Michael, my late husband, who set me off. He was as much a foodie as I am and my Taster. Together we planned this book.

Jewish people are being exposed to modern stylish cooking but not modern stylish kosher cooking. In my book *Modern Jewish Cooking With Style* I capture and interpret these influences and remove the obstacles.

Today, mass media enthusiasm for cooking prevails. Television has made celebrities of talented chefs. Newspapers and magazines have regular cookery columns. New cookery books are being published highlighting the latest style and cooking methods. Restaurants are continuously creating new eating experiences.

All my recipes follow the dietary Laws of Kashrut. Many can be made for Passover or changed from meat to parev. With parev cooking in mind, I have tested dairy substitutes such as soya milk to ensure that they work. Our traditions and festivals have not been ignored.

You can use these recipes in many ways – as a good read, to plan stylish dinner parties, to create a simple supper for your family, to execute large scale entertaining and to bring new style to festive meals.

In *Modern Jewish Cooking With Style* the recipes are clear, detailed and include timing guides. Many dishes can be prepared in advance in stages, frozen and reheated in the microwave. All ingredients are on the supermarket shelves.

These recipes really work – they have been tested by friends and family – cooks not chefs!

I want you to use the recipes as a guide. You will also find unusual ingredients. Feel free to mix and match for variety and to allow for the tastes and allergies of those you are cooking for.

Cooking should be a fun and pleasurable experience – not a mad rush and eleventh-hour panic. I make particular reference to planning ahead and organising yourself – from your shopping list to the final garnish and choice of wine.

I have written *Modern Jewish Cooking With Style* with the sincere desire to share my love of cooking. I hope my book will inspire you!

Enjoy!

Denise Phillips

Notes on Recipes

- *Both imperial and metric measurements are given.* Use either set of quantities but not a mixture in any one recipe.

- *For your convenience, I have broken many of the recipes down into stages.* This will enable you to prepare, freeze and/or cook parts of a dish to suit your own time management. I hope that this will make some of the more intricate recipes more achievable if time is short.

- *Only freeze those dishes that are so indicated.* Cool to room temperature as quickly as possible (decanting into smaller dishes will speed this process). Complete the cooling in the fridge. Always label and date food clearly before it goes in the freezer to prevent UFOs (unidentified frozen objects).

- *Each recipe has been given approximate preparation and cooking times.* The preparation time includes weighing, peeling, chopping, sautéing, rolling out – in fact, everything that is 'hands on' or requires close attention before the main cooking.

- *Cooking time is the length of time when the dish (or parts of the dish) can be left in the oven, under a grill or on a hob unattended.* Set a timer to remind you to check. During this time you may be able to prepare other parts of the dish or meal, which will speed up the total time taken to complete the recipe. Multi-tasking in the kitchen needs concentration and planning at first, but it will bring its own rewards.

● *Finally, before starting to cook, I offer the following advice.* First, read through both the list of ingredients and the method, including timing information and alternatives. Second, locate and have ready everything you will need before you start. Having ingredients measured and the correct equipment to hand will make the whole experience faster and more efficient.

Ingredients

- All the ingredients are kosher. Some 'milky' recipes may be made parev by substituting ingredients detailed in the recipes. Dishes suitable for Pesach are indicated, as are any substitute ingredients.

- Try to use fresh, organic produce when it is in season, where possible, as this will give the best flavour. If fresh herbs are not available, dried or frozen can be substituted in cooked dishes, but halve the quantities.

- Eggs are large, unless stated otherwise.

- Butter is always unsalted, unless stated otherwise.

- To season, use sea salt and freshly ground black pepper.

- All spoon measurements are level unless stated otherwise.

1

Planning and Presentation

I feel that presentation is
extremely important in cooking
and have therefore listed some
easy to follow guide-lines to
make even the most simple of dishes
more appetising. All my recipes
describe serving food stylishly
to impress your guests!

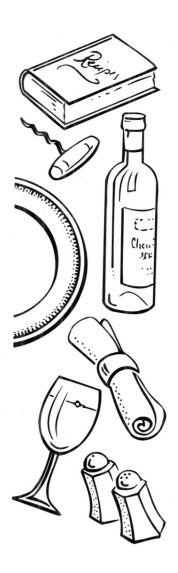

Planning Your Menu

Deciding what to cook and in what combination is often the hardest part of entertaining. There have been many times, probably, when you have browsed through numerous cookbooks looking for inspiration, only to return to the old tried-and-tested favourites. I hope that the recipes in this book will encourage you to experiment with new ideas.

When planning your dinner party, first decide which main course you wish to serve and then work out the rest of the menu, bearing in mind the following:

- *Cooking methods*. Do not serve a fried starter with a fried main course.

- *Variety of ingredients*. Avoid making tomato soup followed by a main course of tuna with tomato salsa.

- *Variety of tastes*. Too many flavours will spoil the main ingredient. Too many distinct tastes numb the palate, leading to confusion.

- *Colour*. If all the main ingredients are one colour, the final dish may taste delicious but appear incredibly dull, unless you are deliberately cooking for a themed occasion such as a black-and-white dinner.

- *Texture*. Use a variety of textures throughout the meal: smooth followed by crunchy; chewy followed by melt-in-the-mouth.

- *Season*. Every ingredient tastes better when it is naturally available. Strawberries in winter cannot be compared with summer fruit.

- *Balance of light and heavy*. A filling main course may not require a starter. Three courses are not always necessary. For a change, consider a selection of canapés instead of a starter.

- *Age and sex of your guests*. Most children, the elderly and women tend to have smaller appetites than teenagers and

men. Consider, too, their preferences for different types
of food.

- *Eggs*. Avoid too many eggs in a meal. Soufflé followed by
  a quiche and then a custard has far too much egg content.

- *Rich food*. The best way to check for nutritional balance is
  to look through the ingredients for each course,
  identifying the fat, cream or butter content and ensuring
  that they do not appear in large amounts in more than one
  dish. Remember, also, to maintain the balance between
  animal protein, vegetables, fibre, fruits, sugars and
  vitamins.

To help you choose well-balanced menus for specific
occasions, here are a few examples.

Seder night (meat)
Shredded Carrot and Celeriac Soup

Honey Glazed Chicken Breast with Fondant Potatoes

Lime Mousse or Double Chocolate Baked Alaska

Seder night (milk)
Colourful Goat's Cheese Terrine

Mediterranean Salmon Fillet, New Potatoes and Spinach

Fruits of the Forest Crème Brûlée

Informal summer supper (meat)
Rosemary Ciabatta
Summer Pea Soup

Crunchy Chicken Pecan Salad

Cinnamon Toast with Hot Cherries
and Ice Cream

Autumn sophisticated Saturday night dinner (milk)

Mozzarella and Spinach Choux Bites
Black Olive and Cheese Pastry Balls

Haddock and Orange Terrine
Asparagus and Spring Onion Millefeuille
with Grilled Vegetables

Crunchy Nut Biscotti with Red Fruits
Bread and Butter Pudding with
Greek Yoghurt and Honey

Rosh Hashanah family lunch (meat)

Roasted Butternut Squash Soup

or

Chicken Liver Caesar Salad

Spatchcock of Poussin with
Caramelised Apples, Fondant Potatoes,
Carrot and Courgette Ribbons

Lacy Vanilla Apple Pie with Custard
Hot Chocolate Soufflé

Shavuot family lunch (milk)

Penne and Parmesan Frittata

Best-ever Fish Pie

Individual Raspberry Cheesecakes

Informal weekday supper with friends (Meat)

Marinated Tuna with Balsamic Vinegar

Pappardelle Pasta with Smoked Turkey,
Fennel and Orange

Brandy, Date and Coffee Pudding
with Kahlua Zabaglione

Entertaining to impress
Canapés
Sushi Selection
Oriental Chicken
Filo Tarts
Wild Mushroom Rolls
Sherry Black Bean Soup
or
Spicy Mushroom and Lemon Grass Soup
Sesame and Orange Lamb Chops with Sweet Potato
Chunky Chips and Steamed Greens
Thin Pear Pastries with Parev
Hazelnut Ice Cream or Soya Custard

Stylish Party Planning Made Simple

The thought of cooking for more than eight people may be daunting. This is easily overcome by careful, serious organisation. The best way to handle the situation is to think ahead, plan ahead and cook in stages.

Handy hints and tips

- It is always much easier to use recipes that you have used before. If you are keen to use a new recipe, try it out beforehand.

- Check the menu against the pots, pans, oven space, hob burners, freezer and refrigeration space that you will need to produce it.

- Make a timetable, bearing in mind that larger quantities take longer and may require additional cooking time.

- Scaling recipes up and down is not always only a matter of doubling or halving the ingredients. Large stews may need proportionately less liquid than small ones. Doubling up on powerful spices like chilli, paprika and saffron is often too much for the dish, so use sparingly. Rich or strong ingredients like onions, blue cheese, wine, double cream, mustard and vinegars do not always need doubling up. Err on the cautious side — you can always add but it is much harder to take away.

- Liquid recipes cooked at or about boiling point will take a little longer for the water to come to the boil, but after that the larger volume should make no difference to the cooking time.

- Large roasts or cakes will take longer to cook but will require a a lower temperature if the heat is to penetrate without burning the outside to a crisp.

- Heating food from the refrigerator will take longer than from room temperature and a moderate heat of 180°C (350°F/gas mark 4) should be used.

- To keep food warm use a low temperature — 150°C (300°/gas mark 2) or a double-boiler.

- Hotplates for hot dishes are very useful for large gatherings especially for buffet service.

- Plan your shopping as well as your cooking. Non-perishables can be bought well in advance. Perishables should be bought nearer the event — watch the sell-by dates. Fruit and vegetables are obviously best if bought as fresh as possible. Use local delivery services where available. Extended supermarket opening times and on-line shopping by computer are very useful for the busy cook.

- When catering for more than 8–10 people, it is much easier to make and serve two or three batches of the same dish than it is to make an one large one. For example, lasagne for 20 in one dish is very difficult to cook and serve with style.

Choosing Wine

Choosing wine for a dinner party is very much a personal decision. Traditionally, white wine is served with fish and red wine with meat. However, this can be rather limiting and does not leave much room for personal taste and preference. Here are some guidelines and advice on how to get the most enjoyment from your wine with your meal.

Buying and storing wine

- One bottle of wine serves 5–6 glasses. Buy half bottles of wine if your guests are not big drinkers. Half bottles are also useful if you want to serve a different wine with each course.

- Store wine where there is a constant temperature of about 11°C (52°F). An ideal location is in a wine rack in a fitted cupboard that is not used often. Under the stairs, which may frequently be disturbed or in a garage, where the temperature fluctuates widely between winter and summer, are not good places.

- Store bottles lying on their sides. If they are stored upright, the cork might dry out and become brittle, causing it to contract inside the bottle. This would consequently allow air into the wine and, if it becomes oxidised, the wine goes off.

- The best way to open a bottle of wine is to cut the seal back from the neck so that the metal does not come into contact with the wine when it is poured. To open a bottle of sparkling wine, take the bottle with one hand holding the cork with a tea towel and twist with the other.

Decanting and serving wine

- There are several good reasons for decanting wine. First, it helps to remove the sediment and ensures that you can safely pour the entire contents without spoiling it with wine deposits. Second, most red wines benefit from exposure to air before drinking – the bouquet and flavour of the wine start to breathe, which intensifies the overall taste. Finally, a cheap bottle of good red wine suddenly appears much more expensive if it is poured from a cut-glass decanter – just as a glass of wine tastes better in a crystal glass than a paper cup.

- If you are serving a selection of wine, start with white and continue with red.

- The convention is to begin a meal with dry wine and complete it with sweet. Similarly, begin with the lightest-bodied wine and finish with the fullest-bodied.

- White wine is served in tulip-shaped glasses. Fill the glass to nearly three-quarters full. If you overfill, the wine loses its chill quickly. Red wine glasses have fatter bowls (balloon) and the serving should be bigger.

- Wine will last approximately 3-4 days once opened. There are various wine-savers available but all wines should be consumed within this time.

- Most people believe that red wines should be served at room temperature but, in fact, this can vary quite considerably. I recommend that red wine should be left open in the room in which it is to be served for at least 4 hours. I regularly serve Burgundies somewhat cooler. However, there are some red wines, such as Beaujolais, that are better served chilled. Its fruity taste is enhanced if it has spent an hour or so in the refrigerator.

- White wines taste better if they are served chilled. Sweeter whites should be served cooler than dry ones.

The different varieties of wine

Below is a list that explains the different styles of wine. I have given some suitable variations because all too often people become familiar with a specific variety or grape and are reluctant to try something new.

Red wines

Clarets

There are three different types of claret.

1 A light, blackcurranty Cabernet-style. The Cabernet Sauvignon and Merlot grapes are the most popular wine varieties used by red wine makers. The Red Bordeaux provides the model wine but the lightest, freshest styles are from the Loire Valley. *Alternatives* – Cabernet Franc or Gamay Chianti (Italy).

2 Full, rich, blackcurrant, often aged in oak. *Alternative* – Cabernet Sauvignon.

3 Big plummy reds – these are from Bordeaux, mostly from Merlot grapes grown in Pomerol and St. Emilion. *Alternatives* – Merlot and Cabernet Sauvignon, red Zinfandel (USA), Shiraz (Australia).

Light and fruity Beaujolais

Beaujolais is the best known of the light, fruity, fresh reds to be drunk almost immediately. *Alternatives* – wines based on the Gamay grape, young Zinfandel (USA), young style Shiraz (Australia).

Burgundy

A light simple style red wine. The grape is Pinot noir.

Rosés

These wines have similar characteristics to red wines, but are lighter, and more tangy and fruity. Traditionally, they are made by crushing red grapes and letting them steep in their colourless juice for a few hours, so that a little of the skin colour seeps out. The juice is then fermented in chilled tanks to keep it fresh. Rosés are best served chilled. Rosés come mainly from Anjou, the Rhône and Provence. The Cabernet Franc grape and Coteaux du Tricastin are very popular.

White wines

Light Chablis-type whites — these are mainly made from the Chardonnay grape in the lighter, cool climate of Chablis. *Alternatives* — Chardonnay wines from Chile and USA, and Chenin Blanc (USA) are excellent.

Fuller, 'oaky' white burgundy types — these are wines that have gained their richness and vanilla from maturing in oak barrels. The grape variety is Chardonnay. *Alternatives* — Chardonnay wines produced in Israel.

German or 'fruity' — these are wines based on grapes that are to a greater or lesser degree, aromatic and perfumed. The grape varieties Riesling or Alsace Rieslings are good examples.

Perfumed, dry grape — Alsace Gewurztraminer is quite an acquired taste.

Perfumed medium grape — the grape is mostly Muller-Thurgau and Niersteiner Gutes Domtal. *Alternative* — Welschriesling (Austria).

Light 'green' whites — these are tangy, sharp whites, generally drunk young. The grape varieties are mainly Sancerre and Sauvignon Blanc. *Alternatives* — Sauvignon blanc from the Loire, USA and Australia.

Champagne

There are no alternatives to the true, dry Champagne. However, Asti Spumante from Italy, Crémant d'Alsace and Vouvray are great, but much sweeter, sparkling wines.

Sweet dessert wines
The Sauternes and Muscats are rich, sweet, full-bodied wines that have a flavour of orange marmalade.
Alternatives — Tokay (Hungarian), Last Harvest Johannesburg Riesling (USA).

The Three Golden Rules of Presentation

1 *Keep it simple* — over-garnished or elaborately decorated food rarely appeals.

2 *Keep it fresh* — nothing looks more off-putting than tired food.

3 *Keep it relevant* — a sprig of fresh watercress complements lamb cutlets perfectly, because the texture, taste and colour all enhance the lamb. However, scratchy sprigs of parsley, although providing colour, do not highlight the lamb and are unpleasant to eat.

Making the Most of Presentation

Centre height
Stacking certain foods to create a finished dish with height can turn the ordinary into something very special. For example, the layered Aubergine Schnitzel (see p.164-165) is an aesthetically pleasing tower of colour.

Contrasting Rows
Biscuits, petit fours and canapés look most attractive when arranged in neat rows. Combine one or two complementary colours and vary tastes and textures to create appetising and appealing food.

Variety

Each mouthful should be an interesting combination of texture and flavour. Think carefully about the blend of different textures, tastes and flavours.

Diagonal Lines

Diamond shapes and diagonal lines are easier to achieve than straight ones.

Dusting

Dusting a plate with paprika, icing sugar or cocoa powder gives an elegant finishing touch.

Colour

The colour of food can be as important as the taste. Consider the use of matching or contrasting food and tableware. Black and white plain crockery dishes do not detract from food, whilst highly patterned plates could spoil the finished effect.

Contrasting the simple and the elaborate

If the dish or bowl is elaborately decorated, contrastingly simple food lends itself to showing the design to the best advantage.

Uneven numbers

As a rule, use uneven numbers to display food. As with flower arranging, this makes it more pleasing to the eye.

A balanced look

Do not be mean – serve a generous portion but avoid over-filling plates to use everything up. This can be messy and off-putting. It is better to leave that little bit extra in the dish, rather than cramming it on the plate; your guests can always return for more.

Overlapping

Sliced meats, steaks, terrines, etc. look best evenly overlapping and more can be fitted comfortably on the plate.

Best side uppermost

Usually the side of meat, or fish which has been grilled or fried first should be presented uppermost. Bones are generally unsightly and, if they cannot be clipped off or removed, should be tucked away out of sight.

Witty foods

It is sometimes amusing and attractive to produce food that raises a smile or intrigues the diner, for example, try a sparkler in the Double-chocolate Baked Alaska (see p.181) as a spectacular finale to a birthday dinner.

2

The Secrets of the Successful Cook

In this chapter I explain some specific cooking techniques. All too often we shy away from soufflés or pastry-making because of past disasters or misconceptions about how difficult they are to do. My guidelines will be your check list to learn new skills – I hope that you enjoy the challenge.

Handy Cooking Tips

- When preheating the oven, always heat it to a temperature higher than you need. The minute you open the oven door the heat drops. But do remember to turn the oven down to the correct temperature once the dish is in.

- Rearrange the oven trays to the appropriate depth and number of shelves before you turn on the oven. Moving them around when they are hot is both tricky and dangerous – you can easily burn yourself. In addition, the longer the oven door is open the more heat you lose.

- Use base heat where possible. This means heating up a baking tray on which you can place your food or dish to speed up the cooking process. Very few ovens have completely constant, all round temperatures.

- If some egg shell accidentally falls into the bowl when cracking an egg use another piece of shell to retrieve it. The egg shell acts as a magnet and it is much quicker than chasing it around with a spoon.

- When you invite your guests, check out their strong dislikes or allergies. This prevents you from wasting your time on something they cannot eat and spares their embarrassment.

- Always taste food at the end of cooking before adding the final seasoning. Flavours develop and change throughout the cooking process. In particular, too much salt at the beginning can spoil the complete dish or prevent the true flavours of the specific ingredients from coming through.

- Every now and again, go shopping when you are not in a rush and just browse at the shelves you normally whizz past. New ingredients or ideas can be really inspiring – give yourself time to look.

Cooking Pasta

- All pasta should be cooked until al dente, still firm to the bite, but without a hard centre. The only way to check if pasta is cooked is to taste it!

- For a main course, allow 100g (3½oz) of pasta per person.

- Always add pasta to a large saucepan containing plenty of boiling water, with 2tsp of salt. Cook the pasta at a fast rolling boil to prevent sticking. Never leave pasta for longer than required in the boiling water, otherwise it goes very soggy.

- Fresh pasta will be cooked by the time it takes the water to return to a full boil. Dried pasta will take longer and will depend upon its shape and size. Keep back a few tablespoons of the cooking water from the drained pasta. This helps the sauce to cling to the pasta.

- In general, chunky sauces are best with chunky pastas such as spirals, penne, shells or rigatoni. Thin, more fluid sauces suit long thin pastas such as linguine, tagliatelle, pappardelle, spaghetti or angel hair.

Making Stocks

- The secret of a good stock is slow, gentle simmering.

- Skimming, especially for meat stocks, is vital as fat and scum rise to the surface. Remove the scum with a perforated spoon every 10–15 minutes.

- Vegetables and bones should be evenly well-browned, but not burned, to make a good brown stock.

- Cooked bones are less satisfactory than raw bones as they have lost a great deal of their flavour already.

- The longer meat and poultry stocks are simmered, the better the flavour.

- As vegetable stocks contain very little fat, simmering for one hour is generally enough.

- Fish stocks need a maximum of 30 minutes simmering. Too much cooking will result in the fishbones releasing a bitter flavour.

- Do not add salt until the end as it does not boil off with the water but remains in the pan.

Chicken stock
Makes 2.25 l (4 pints)

1.5kg (3lb 3oz) fresh chicken
1 medium onion stuck with 3 cloves
2 medium carrots, peeled and coarsely sliced
2 medium leeks, washed and coarsely sliced
1 head of garlic, unpeeled
6 sprigs of fresh flat-leaf parsley, with stems
3 sprigs of fresh thyme
1 bay leaf
pinch of salt
3 litres (5½ pints) cold water to cover by at least 7.5cm (3in)

1 Place all the ingredients in a saucepan or stockpot. Cover and bring slowly to the boil. Reduce heat to a gentle simmer. Skim off any scum. Simmer very gently with the saucepan partially covered for 2–3 hours, skimming from time to time.

2 Strain, being careful not to force any of the ingredients through the sieve. Cool thoroughly before refrigerating.

3 Skim off any fat and use or freeze until needed.

Fish Stock

Makes: 2 litres (3½ pints)

1 kg (2lb 2oz) fish bones, heads and trimmings from non-oily fish.
  broken up and rinsed under cold water
1 medium onion, peeled and roughly chopped
2 medium carrots, peeled and coarsely sliced
1 medium leek washed and coarsely sliced,
½ fennel bulb, sliced
3 sprigs of fresh flat-leaf parsley, with stems
3 sprigs of fresh thyme
1 bay leaf
A pinch of salt
2.5 litres (4½ pints) cold water to cover

1 Place all the ingredients in a saucepan or stockpot.

2 Cover and bring slowly to the boil. Reduce heat to a gentle simmer.

3 Skim off any scum.

4 Simmer very gently with the saucepan partially covered for 30 minutes, skimming from time to time.

5 Allow to cool.

6 Strain.

7 Refrigerate or freeze until needed.

Vegetable Stock

Makes: 2.7 litres / 4¾ pints

3 medium onions peeled and roughly chopped
5 medium carrots, peeled and roughly chopped
3 medium leeks, washed and coarsely sliced
3 medium sticks of celery, trimmed and roughly chopped
8 cabbage leaves, sliced
1 head of full flavoured green lettuce, sliced
6 sprigs of fresh flat-leaf parsley, with stems, roughly chopped
3 sprigs of thyme
1 bay leaf
a pinch of salt
3.5 litres (6 pints) cold water to cover

1 Place all the ingredients in a saucepan or stockpot.

2 Cover and bring slowly to the boil.

3 Reduce heat to a gentle simmer.

4 Skim off any scum.

5 Simmer very gently with the lid ajar for one hour, skimming from time to time.

6 Allow to cool.

7 Strain.

8 Refrigerate or freeze until needed.

Making Sauces

A sauce can enhance a dish or swamp its flavours, so make it with care. Underseason first, as you can always add more salt or pepper later. Quite often the full flavour of a sauce does not come through until the end of the cooking. Sauces are thickened in several ways:

- *Roux*. This is a white sauce using butter and flour, used, for example, in the Salmon Pâté en Croûte (see p.129–130).

- *Egg yolks*. These are often used for thickening a custard. Pay attention while cooking as an initial fierce heat will curdle the sauce unless cornflour or plain flour is added to it to stabilise it.

- *Cornflour, plain flour and potato flour*. These can be added to a hot liquid at any stage to thicken the mixture. To do this, add a tablespoon of the sauce, soup or some plain water to the flour. Mix to a paste and add in to the dish.

- *Reducing*. To reduce a sauce, soup, stock or syrup, boil rapidly. This reduces the amount of liquid by evaporation leaving a thickened, more flavoursome, concentrated liquid.

Making a Successful Terrine

The secret of a successful terrine lies in the seasoning. If you are uncertain whether it is seasoned sufficiently, cool a teaspoon of the mixture and then taste.

Cook terrines in a bain-marie to guarantee even cooking. To make a bain-marie, half fill a roasting tin with hot water and place the terrine, in its dish, in the tin to cook. The terrine cooks gently in the steamy atmosphere and is protected from direct heat.

Terrines cut better when they are cold. Use a serrated knife or an electric carving knife for slicing.

Making Soufflés

- Always preheat the oven well in advance so that when the soufflé is ready for cooking it can go straight in. Delay in doing so will cause the egg whites to collapse.

- Always heat up a baking tray to use as a base heat to encourage immediate cooking.

- For sweet soufflés, grease ramekins with butter or margarine and sugar.

- For savoury soufflés, grease ramekins with butter or margarine and breadcrumbs, plain flour, parmesan or ground nuts.

- Overseason the thick base mixture because the addition of egg whites increases the volume and thus reduces the flavouring.

- Make sure the bowl that you use for whisking the egg whites is scrupulously clean. Any trace of fat or grease will prevent their whisking up properly.

- Use a figure of eight movement when mixing the egg whites into the base mixture. A metal spoon is best for this. Add one tablespoon of egg white first, then the rest to loosen the mixture. Do not over-beat at this stage or the air already within the soufflé will escape.

- Avoid opening the oven door while the soufflés are cooking.

- You can freeze soufflés raw once the egg whites have been added. To cook from frozen, increase the cooking time by approximately 25 minutes for a large soufflé and 10 minutes for individual ramekins.

Making Pastry

Filo pastry

As this dries out very quickly, always keep it covered with a damp tea towel or cling film. Brush the sheets pastry of with fat to bind them together and give flavour and colour. Melted butter is best. For a parev option use margarine and egg yolk: combine 30g (1oz) cooled, melted margarine with 1 beaten egg yolk (if the margarine is too hot, it will cook the yolk).

Hot water pastry

This is probably one of the easiest pastries to make. For this pastry, water and fat are heated together and mixed into the flour. As there is a high proportion of water, the pastry will be quite hard, which makes it perfect for a pie with lots of juice as it prevents leakage. The fat used is generally lard, which can be vegetarian lard. Always add a good pinch of salt as lard lacks flavour.

Do not allow the water to boil before the fat has melted. If the water reduces by boiling, the proportion of water to flour will not be correct. Mix the water and melted fat into the flour quickly and keep the pastry in a bowl, covered with a hot damp cloth or cling film. This prevents the fat becoming set and the pastry flaking and drying out, which makes it unmanageable. You can roll and reroll this pastry without spoiling the final result.

Choux pastry

This pastry, containing eggs and butter, is easy to make. Follow the recipe exactly and remember to:

- Measure the ingredients exactly.

- Not let the water boil until the butter has melted. When the butter has melted, bring the mixture immediately to a full rolling boil.

- Have the flour ready in a bowl so that the minute your rolling boil is achieved, you can tip in the flour, all in one go.

- Not to overbeat; once the mixture is leaving the sides of the pan, stop.

- Cool before adding the egg – too much heat will scramble the eggs.

- Only beat in enough egg to reach a dropping consistency. If the mixture is too stiff, the pastry will be stodgy. If it is too sloppy, it will rise unevenly into shapeless, hard lumps.

- Bake on a baking tray lined with damp baking parchment – the steam helps the paste to rise.

- Bake until it is evenly browned, otherwise the inside of the pastry will be uncooked.

- Split the buns, or poke holes in them with a skewer, to allow the steam inside to escape if the pastry is to be served cold. If the steam remains trapped, the pastry will be soggy and a little heavy.

- Serve the pastry on the day it is made, or store frozen. It will not keep well in a tin.

3

Ingredients for the Stylish Cook

Keeping a well-stocked store cupboard is
all part of managing a busy cook's
lifestyle. I often buy several packets of
kosher gelatine when I am in the local
kosher grocer store as it's a good product
with a long sell-by date that is not
available at the supermarket. This means
that there is no excuse not to
quickly create a
delicious terrine or mousse.
Here I look at a variety
of essential and unusual ingredients,
and I hope that I will encourage
you to try something new.

Lentils

Although lentils grow in pods, they are always sold podded and dried.

- Red lentils have a pleasant mild flavour and cook down easily to a purée. They are often used in Indian cooking to make dhal and other mildly spiced dishes. They are used in soups, stews, sauces and salads.
- Green Puy lentils are dark green seeds with blue marbling and have an excellent flavour.
- Green lentils, from Haute-Loire have thinner skins but a similar flavour.
- Brown lentils do not break up during cooking and are often mixed with small pasta shapes or rice for a contrast of flavours and textures. They make the perfect bed for cooked meats and are delicious served cold and dressed with olive oil.
- Blonde lentils are oval and flat and grown in the Cantal, France.

Cook's Tip

Lentils will absorb the flavours of whatever they are cooked with, so add any appropriate herbs or spices to the cooking liquid.

Capers

Capers are the immature flower buds of a wild Mediterranean shrub. They are pickled in white wine vinegar or preserved in brine which gives them a piquant, peppery flavour.

Sicilian capers are packed in whole salt, which should be rinsed off before using the capers.

Caper berries look like large, fat capers on long stalks, but they are actually the fruit of the caper shrub. They can be served as a cocktail snack or in salads.

Culinary Uses

Capers are mainly used as a condiment or garnish but they also add great flavour to fish dishes, salads, pizzas, pasta and sauces.

Buying and Storing

Choosing pickled or brined capers is a matter of taste, as is whether or not you rinse the vinegar off before use.

Large capers are usually cheaper than small capers; there is no difference in flavour but the small capers often make a more attractive garnish.

Salt-packed capers should be used as soon as possible. Once opened, jars of capers should be kept in the fridge and covered with the preserving liquid.

Gelatine

People tend to shy away from using recipes with gelatine but, once you have mastered a few golden rules, hopefully you will experiment with a wide variety of sweet and savoury dishes. Kosher gelatine comes in individual sachets. It is a parev powder made from fish bones, with no added colour or preservatives.

- Always weigh your gelatine accurately. One packet or 7g (¼oz) of gelatine will set 200ml (7fl oz) of liquid. However, do check the packet instructions. Too much gelatine and the food will taste rubbery; too little and it may fail to set.

- Soak the gelatine into a measured amount of liquid (never the other way round) so that it can start to 'sponge', or dissolve.

- Warm the gelatine and liquid gently in a saucepan but do not allow it to boil or it will go stringy and unusable.

- Only add the gelatine-based mixture to the other ingredients when it is on the point of setting. If the mixture is not cool enough, the ingredients will not set.

Rice

Without a doubt, rice is the world's grain of choice: nutritious, inexpensive and versatile. Rice is classified as long, medium and short grain. Medium and short grain rices include risotto, pudding, and sticky Japanese sushi rice. Other rices include brown, red, flaked — and wild rice which is not really rice at all.

Allow 50g (2oz) raw rice per person. If the recipe asks for a certain quantity of cooked rice, use half that amount of raw.

Long grain rice

- American long grain was once known as Carolina rice as it was first cultivated in South Carolina, USA.

- Basmati rice is the longest grained Indian rice. Its name means 'whose nature it is to be aromatic'. The finest Basmati grows on the lower slopes of the Himalayas, watered by the melted snow from the high peaks. It has a special nutty flavour that makes it a perfect accompaniment to curries and other exotic foods.

- Thai fragrant or jasmine rice has a slightly sticky quality that makes it easy to eat with chopsticks. It is, therefore, particularly used for oriental dishes such as Thai, Indonesian and Chinese.

Medium and short grain rice

- Risotto rice is a medium grain rice that must be stirred during cooking to release the starch. This thickens the cooking liquid to a rich, gooey consistency. It absorbs more liquid than long grain rice so use 1l (1¾ pints) stock to 300-350g (10-12oz) rice.

- Arborio rice from Italy's Po Valley is the best-known and is a long grain rice, whereas Carnaroli and Vialone Nano are medium grains.

- Valencia rice is a short grain rice grown outside Valencia in Spain and is traditionally used for paella.

- Pudding rice is particularly good for milk puddings. Make sure that you use plenty of milk so that the plump grains produce a creamy consistency. Risotto rice can also be used.

- Japanese rice is popular in South-east Asia for its sweetish flavour and sticky texture.

Other rices

- Brown rice has had its outer husk removed, leaving the bran in place. It is chewier and higher in fibre than white rice and needs at least twice as much cooking.

- Red rice comes from the Camargue in the south of France. It is a grain once regarded as a weed, which was then cross-fertilised with the local rice to produce a novelty rice.

- Wild rice is not really a rice but the seeds of an aquatic grass that once grew wild around the lakes of North America. It is now cheaper and more readily available than it used to be. You can also buy it combined with other rices.

To flavour long grain rice

- Add lemon juice, lime juice, lime leaves or a strip of lemon zest to the cooking water.

- Add cracked cardamom pods, saffron threads, cinnamon sticks or turmeric for colour.

- Cook in half water and half coconut milk for a real aromatic effect.

- Add butter and olive oil at the end of cooking. This enriches the final taste.

Cooking rice

- Long grain rice absorbs twice its volume of water during cooking.

- Add a tablespoon of butter or oil to the water when cooking rice to keep the grains separate.

- Simmer rice in stock for more flavour.

- Don't stir simmering rice (except risotto); this releases the starch, which will make the rice sticky.

- If simmered rice is cooked but still watery, fluff it with a fork over a low heat to evaporate the water.

- Simmer rice in a heavy saucepan so that the rice at the bottom does not scorch, and also make sure that the pan is big enough, as rice triples in bulk when cooked.

- Cooking rice in a high concentration of acid such as tomatoes or orange juice slows its ability to absorb water, so extra liquid and possibly extra cooking time may be needed.

- Fluff the rice with a fork before serving as this helps the grains to separate.

Unusual spices and herbs

Hot red chillies and cool red peppers are all part of the same capsicum family, although this is sometimes hard to believe. Fresh chillies come in various colours and sizes. They all have some degree of 'heat' so read the label carefully or taste cautiously to ensure you achieve the desired 'kick' to your cooking. The main source of heat is in the inside membrane and the seeds, so discard these and use just the flesh. Wear gloves when handling or wash your hands thoroughly immediately after using chillies. The heat lingers and can be transferred to burn your skin or, even worse, your eyes.

Chili powder, spelt with a single 'l' indicates a blend of chillies, cumin, oregano, salt and garlic. This gives a characteristic flavour to Texan-style dishes such as chilli con carne. Chilli powder, spelt with a double 'll' means the powder only contains pure ground chillies.

Cayenne pepper is made from the pure ground chillies of the smaller, more pungent capsicums grown in India, Africa, Mexico, China and Japan. Paprika is the mildest form of chilli with a flavour of red peppers and no fiery heat. It traditionally comes from Hungary and used in many Hungarian dishes.

Saffron is the orange stigma of the autumn crocus. It is the world's most valuable and expensive spice. Good saffron is less than one year old and its threads are a brilliant orange colour. It has a musky fragrance and a pungent, mildly bitter taste and gives a beautiful, yellowy-orange tint to food. Substitutes such as safflower, marigold and tumeric may be used but they only provide the colour and not the unique taste of saffron.

Today, about 70% of saffron comes from Spain. Its quality is measured according to the proportion of crimson threads to yellow ones. Coupé is the most powerful grade, followed by Mancha Selecto, then Rio and finally Sierra. When cooking with saffron, the longer it infuses in the liquid, the stronger the colour – so infuse for an hour rather than 10 minutes before cooking. It is ideal in soups, bread, biscuits, sauces, risottos and rice dishes, mashed potato, fish dishes, tagines, ice creams – and even chicken soup.

Most whole spices lose some of their pungency after a long time in packaging. To revive them, roast whole in a preheated oven at 180°C (350°F/gas mark 4) for 5 minutes. When their aroma becomes noticeable, remove from the oven and use according to the recipe. Alternatively, fry ground spices in a frying pan to release their flavour. As a general rule, whole spices have a better flavour if you grind them freshly yourself.

Juniper berries are the fruit of a small evergreen shrub. These small berries are purple when fresh and dark brown when dried. When they are crushed, they release a spicy flavour. They are best used in marinades for fish, meat, poultry and beef, soups casseroles and vegetable stews.

Nutmeg is the sweet nutty spicy seed of the nutmeg tree. Use it to flavour mashed potato, soufflés, spinach, casseroles, soups and rice puddings. You can buy nutmeg whole or ground, although the ground spice tends to lose its flavour quite quickly.

Star anis are eight pointed stars from a tree of the Magnolia family. They have a slightly sweet, liquorice flavour and are available whole or ground. Use them in stocks, soups, breads, cakes and stews.

Lemon grass is an indispensable ingredient in Thai cuisine. It is a straw-like stalk that has a woody, lemony flavour. Lemon grass helps to accent everything from hot and sour soups such as the Spicy Mushroom and Lemon Grass Soup (see p.72) to chicken, fish or curries. To use, remove the few outer layers from the lower part and sauté the chopped inner fibre. The stalks will last quite well for 2–3 weeks in a refrigerator and chopped lemon grass can be put in a plastic bag and frozen. You can buy dried lemon grass but fresh is best. It is now available in small jars ready to use.

Lime leaves are the dark green, glossy leaves of the kaffir lime and impart a pungent, lemon-lime flavour. They are available from oriental shops and specialist supermarkets. The fresh leaves keep well and can be frozen. You can also buy them dried.

Lemon thyme is very similar to traditional thyme but has a distinct lemon flavour. It works very well in soups and stews such as the Basque-style Tuna Stew (see p.158-159). It is easy to grow but is available in some supermarkets.

Oils and Fats

With such a wide variety of oils and fats available, confusion often arises. This guide explains the range of oils and fats and what to use them for.

Olive oils

Olive oil is graded according to acidity; the higher the grade of oil, the lower the level of acidity. The better the olive oil, the stronger the flavour and deeper the colour – these are more appropriate for enhancing food rather than cooking with it.

- Extra virgin olive oil is the first cold pressed olive oil, which means it is the product of first time the green olives are pressed in cold conditions. It tends to be a darker green colour than the other olive oils and is best used cold or gently warmed for dressings, marinades, drizzling over grilled fish, vegetables and risottos. Most extra virgin oils are blended – oils from different estates are mixed for a consistent flavour.

- Virgin olive oil has a higher acidity level than extra virgin olive oil. It is still of a high quality and suitable as a condiment or for light cooking.

- Olive oil is extracted by heat before it is refined. It is, therefore, the best for cooking as the flavour is not affected by high temperatures. It is also a lot cheaper to buy. It tends to have a more yellow and lighter colour when compared with extra virgin olive oil, and the flavour is less pungent.

Nut oils

Nut oils are made from roasted nuts that are pressed to release their flavour. Their colour depends on their degree of toasting. These oils are best for flavouring rather than cooking. They are great for dressings, vinaigrettes and drizzled over fresh salads and vegetables. All the nut oils work well mixed with olive oil as part of a dressing.

- Hazelnut oil has quite an intense flavour, so use sparingly. It is used in oriental stir fries as well as dressings.

- Walnut oil has a great flavour and is a pale golden colour. However, it is notorious for going rancid so always keep it in a dry cool place and frequently check the use-by date.

- Sesame oil is available either toasted or untoasted. The untoasted oil has a pale colour and delicate flavour, whereas the toasted oil is a deep brown colour and has a more intense flavour. Both types have a natural affinity with ginger, chilli, lime and tofu.

- Pumpkin oil is produced from the seeds of a unique type of pumpkin ground in Austria. The seeds are carefully roasted and crushed to produce a wonderful rich velvety-thick oil with a toasted aroma, exquisite nutty flavour and dark green colour. This rare oil is greatly valued for its culinary uses. It is perfect drizzled on to cooked pizza or crusty bread, or used as a dressing for salads or pasta with freshly ground black pepper and salt. Alternatively, pour over roasted peppers or mushrooms and leave to marinate before serving.

Cooking oils and fats

- Corn, sunflower and vegetable oil are used every day for deep and shallow frying.

- Groundnut oil is the best oil for deep and shallow frying.

It has a high smoking point, which means it will not burn easily and its neutral taste is not off-putting.

- Butter burns very easily, so when you want a buttery flavour use half butter and half oil as this allows you to fry at a higher temperature.

- Clarified butter is made by warming butter so that the sediment sinks then straining the clear yellow liquid through a cloth. It gives a fabulous flavour.

- Ghee is Indian clarified butter, which is unsalted. It heats to a higher temperature than ordinary butter without burning. Traditionally, rosewater is added to ghee for flavour.

Flavoured oils

These are very simple to make yourself and the best results are obtained by using extra virgin olive oil with your chosen herb or spice. Use a sterilised bottle that has a cork or screw top and insert the unblemished, undamaged and unbruised flavouring of your choice – chillis, cinnamon, lemon, basil, rosemary and peppercorns, for example – and leave for one week to infuse.

Storing oils

Heat and light can oxidise oil, causing it to smell sour and taste rancid. To avoid this, oils are best stored in cool dry places, away from sunlight. If oils are kept in the refrigerator, they may congeal, so give them time to warm up before you mix them into dressings.

Using cream

How cream behaves is relative to its fat content. The higher the fat, the more versatile the cream.

4

Canapés and Starters

Canapés and starters set the scene for the
forthcoming meal. Some of my recipes,
like the trio of salmon risotto and the
chicken liver caesar salad, can be
produced in larger quantities and served
as a main course.

Assorted starters and canapés should
complement each other and look
attractive. If you are serving both canapés
and starters keep these light and offer
small quantities. Over filling your
guests at this early stage is
not a good thing! I personally favour an
interesting variety of canapés followed
by main course and dessert.

Presenting Canapés

As a useful guide for a drinks party of 10–12 people, you will need to serve approximately 8–10 canapés, 4–5 cold savouries and 4–5 sweet bites per person. Canapés should look like 'artistic jewels' so try to make them:

- Small, dainty and neat, not clumsy.

- *Not overfilled.* An overflowing vol au vent case not only looks messy on a tray but the filling is also likely to spill out onto guests' clothes!

- *One bite big.* There is nothing worse that trying to stuff a large canapé all at once into your mouth; it is neither elegant nor sophisticated!

- *Identical to the others of their kind.* In rows, diagonal lines or stacked high in odd numbers. This will give order, elegance and style to the final appearance .

- *Relevantly garnished.* Keep the same flavours throughout. Too many flavours will destroy the overall taste, especially if it is meant to be delicate. For example, Sun-dried Tomato Tartlets (see p.44) should be garnished with tomatoes and the same herbs that are in the filling.

- *Colour co-ordinated.* The food should match the plates, garnishes, serviettes, flowers, etc. Moreover, pay attention to the room in which the canapés are being served. If the room is blue, then match the blue throughout or use a contrasting but complementary colour for the other items in use.

- *Simple but beautiful.* The use of herbs, flowers, garnishes, baskets, various coloured shaped trays and plates look very attractive but not all at once. Remember the old saying 'less is more'.

- *Fresh.* Only the freshest produce will do. A soggy cucumber or wilted asparagus stick has no place on your canapé tray.

Mini Stuffed Potato Skins

Can be made in advance
Preparation time: *10 minutes*
Cooking time: *20 minutes*

Photograph opposite page 60

1 Preheat the oven to 200°C (400°F/gas mark 6).

2 Boil the the potatoes whole until just tender. Allow to cool for 10 minutes.

3 Cut each potato in half. Scoop out the middle of each potato, using a teaspoon or melon baller. Reserve the scooped-out potato.

4 Place the skins on a baking tray, cut side up, and drizzle with olive oil. Season with salt and freshly ground black pepper. Bake for 15–20 minutes until crispy and remove from oven.

5 Add your chosen fillings and serve hot or cold.

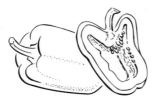

Baby new potatoes
(allow 3 per person)
3 tbs olive oil
salt and freshly ground
black pepper

Suggested fillings
Meat
— *thick Bolognese sauce*
— *shepherd's pie, using the
scooped out potato for the
mashed potato topping*
— *curried chicken*
— *turkey and cranberry sauce*

Milk
— *ripe Brie, black grapes and
toasted almonds*
— *cream cheese, chives and
tinned tuna*

Parev
— *guacamole*
— *smoked salmon and black
pepper or a sprig of dill*
— *hummus and red pepper*
— *garden pea and cumin purée,
made with puréed peas and
ground cumin, a little extra
virgin oil and salt and pepper.
Garnish with cumin seeds*

39

Black Olive and Cheese Pastry Balls

Can be made in advance
Will freeze
Parev option
Preparation time: *20 minutes*
Cooking time: *20 minutes, plus 30 minutes for the pastry to chill*

Serves *15–20 (makes*
approximately 35 balls)

255g (9oz) plain flour
140g (5oz) unsalted butter or
margarine
1 medium egg
155g (5½oz) Gruyère cheese or
strong Cheddar cheese
1 tsp dried cumin or dried
coriander
1 x 400g (14oz) tin black olives,
pitted and drained

Parev option
3 tbs mixed fresh herbs (such as
basil, parsley, coriander),
chopped

These quick and tasty cheese pastry canapés are ideal for a kiddush and are not too filling before a meal. If you prefer, replace the olives with dried apricots or shelled whole almonds.

1 Preheat the oven to 220°C (430°F/gas mark 6).

2 To make the cheese pastry, combine all the ingredients except the olives in a food processor. For the parev option, use the mixed herbs instead of the cheese and margarine instead of butter. Add 2–3 tbs cold water to bring the dough together into a ball. Flatten the pastry ball and wrap in cling film. Chill in the fridge for 30 minutes.

3 Roll out the pastry quite thinly on a lightly floured surface. Using a 5cm (2in) round cutter, cut out circles of pastry. Place a black olive in the centre of each circle. Cover the olive with the pastry and roll to form a small ball. (You can open-freeze the pastry balls at this stage, layered between pieces of clingfilm.)

4 Line a baking tray with baking parchment. Put all the balls on the tray and cook in a pre-heated oven for 15–20 minutes until golden. To cook from frozen, bake for 20–30 minutes.

5 Serve immediately in a basket lined with salad or cabbage leaves.

Sushi Selection

Can be made in advance
Parev option
Preparation time: *40 minutes*
Cooking time: *15 minutes, plus 25 minutes soaking time*

Photograph opposite page 60

Making sushi is much easier than you think and well worth a try. It is really just a matter of assembling all the various ingredients together. The term 'sushi' is a corruption of 'sumeshi', meaning vinegared rice, which is the basis of all sushi dishes.

Assorted fillings

Prepare your chosen fillings first before you make the vinegared rice. These can be made in advance, up to a day before serving. The exception to this is the fresh fish filling, which must be prepared and eaten the same day.

Omelette filling

1 Beat the eggs in a bowl. Add the caster sugar and salt and mix well.

2 Heat the oil in a frying pan. Pour in two-thirds of the egg. Cook over a low heat until just set. Fold the omelette in half in the pan and leave it there.

3 Pour the remaining egg into the clean half of the pan. Cook over a low heat until just set, making sure the flame is under the uncooked egg only. Using a metal spatula, flip the second omelette over the cooked folded one to create a three-layered, semi-circular omelette.

Makes 10–12 sushi pieces

*4–5 sheets roasted nori
   (dried lava paper)*
225g (8oz) sushi rice
500ml (1pint) water
2 tbs sugar
1 tsp salt
2 tbs rice vinegar

To garnish
*wasabi (green horseradish paste
   – if available from specialist
   kosher shops)*
pickled ginger
soy sauce

Omelette filling
3 eggs
1 tbs caster sugar
½ tsp salt
1 tbs vegetable oil

Shiitake mushroom and carrot filling

*3 dried shiitake mushrooms,
   rehydrated and sliced*
*1 medium carrot, peeled and cut
   into julienne strips*
3 tbs caster sugar
3 tbs soy sauce
*3 tbs mirin (Japanese rice wine)
   or dry sherry*

Pepper filling

*1 red and 1 yellow pepper,
   deseeded and cut into
   quarters*
2 tbs olive oil

Raw fish filling

*55g (2oz) weight tuna and/or
   salmon, sliced into thin strips.*

Avocado filling

*1 avocado sliced into strips and
   tossed in lemon juice to
   prevent them discolouring.*

Cucumber filling

*1 cucumber, peeled, deseeded
   and sliced into strips.*

Shiitake mushroom and carrot filling

1   Soak mushrooms in warm water for 25 minutes.
    Drain, reserving 120 ml (4fl oz) of the soaking
    liquid, and squeeze the mushrooms dry. Discard the
    hard stalks and finely shred the mushroom caps.

2   Place the mushrooms, carrot strips, sugar, soy sauce
    and rice wine in a saucepan with the reserved
    soaking liquid. Simmer until all the juices have been
    absorbed.

Pepper filling

Brush the quartered peppers with olive oil and grill skin
side up until the skin starts to blister. Immediately put
the peppers into a bowl and cover with cling film. Slice
the skinned peppers into thin strips.

Vinegared rice

1   Wash the rice thoroughly and drain well in a fine
    sieve.

2   Add the water and cook the rice in a deep saucepan.
    Bring to the boil then simmer, covered, for 15–20
    minutes or until the water is absorbed. Remove
    from the heat, still covered, and leave to stand for
    10 minutes.

4   Place the rice, sugar, salt and vinegar into a bowl
    and mix well. Leave to cool at room temperature
    before using.

To assemble the sushi

1 Put one nori sheet, shortest side closest to you, on a makisu (bamboo mat) or cloth napkin.

2 Spread some vinegared rice over the nori sheet, leaving a 1cm (½in) margin on the edge furthest from you. Using your fingers, press the rice onto the nori sheet.

3 Choose a colourful combination of the 3–4 various fillings and place crossways on the central portion of the rice.

4 Roll up the Makisu from the edge nearest to you so that the ingredients are in the centre of the vinegared rice. Lightly press the rolled Makisu with your fingers.

5 Repeat with more nori and different fillings.

6 Mix together 2 tbs rice vinegar and 1 tbs caster sugar. Dip a sharp knife into the mixture and cut into 10-12 slices. Garnish with wasabi paste (use sparingly), soy sauce and pickled ginger. Refrigerate until ready to serve.

Tuscan Sun-dried Tomato Tartlets with a Herb Filling

Can be made in advance
Will freeze
Preparation time: *20 minutes, plus 30 minutes for the pastry to chill*
Cooking time: *20 minutes*

Makes 35

Pastry
300g (10½oz) plain flour
160g (5½oz) butter
2 sun-dried tomatoes in
*   olive oil, drained*
1 medium egg

Filling
125g (4oz) garlic and
*   herb cream cheese*
125g (4oz) cottage cheese
1 egg
3 tbs finely chopped herbs (such
*   as basil, parsley, mint*
salt and freshly ground
*   black pepper*

To garnish
6 cherry tomatoes, thinly sliced
3 sun-dried tomatoes,
*   thinly sliced*
½ each red and yellow pepper,
*   very finely chopped*
1 small bunch of basil

These tiny Mediterranean-style tartlets are perfect as a little nibble with pre-dinner drinks or to serve at a kiddush.

1   Preheat the oven to 180°C (350°F/gas mark 4).

2   Place all the pastry ingredients in the food processor and mix until a ball of dough is formed. Flatten and wrap in cling film. Refrigerate for 30 minutes.

3   Put all the filling ingredients in the food processor and mix until combined.

4   Roll out the pastry very thinly on a lightly floured surface. Using a 5cm (2in) round, plain cutter, make circles to fit into canapé trays. Line each canapé cup with a pastry circle, easing it in gently. Fill each tartlet with 1 tsp of filling. Bake for 20 minutes.

5   Remove from the oven and garnish with the cherry tomatoes, sun-dried tomatoes, peppers and torn basil leaves.

Roquefort and Sherry Crostini

Can be made in advance
Will freeze (pâté only)
Preparation time: *25 minutes*
Cooking time: *10 minutes*

This strongly-flavoured pâté is wonderfully rich. Instead of crostini, try serving the pâté in a filo basket, on crusty French bread or just as a dip. The pâté is ideal for parties as it can be made in large quantities and frozen. A great way to use up surplus Roquefort!

1 Pre-heat the oven to 200°C (400°F/gas mark 6).

2 Put all the pine nuts into a dry frying pan and cook until golden brown. Set aside.

3 Melt the butter in the same frying pan. Add the red pepper and onion and sauté over a medium heat until the onion is transparent.

4 Transfer the pepper and onion to a food processor and add the cream cheese and kosher blue cheese, mustard, Roquefort and sherry. Process until smooth. Set aside ½oz of the pine nuts for the garnish. Add the rest of pine nuts to the filling mixture and process until well mixed. Use immediately or refrigerate until required.

5 To prepare the crostini, slice the French bread and brush both sides of each slice with olive oil. Place on a baking tray and bake for 10 minutes. Allow to cool before spreading with the pâté.

6 Cut each slice of bread into three and garnish with a sliver of red pepper, pine nuts and thyme.

Makes 35 pieces

55g (2oz) pine nuts
30g (1oz) butter
1 small red pepper, deseeded
  and finely chopped
1 small onion, peeled and
  finely chopped
55g (2oz) cream cheese
55g (2oz) kosher blue cheese
1 tsp Dijon mustard
80g (3oz) Roquefort
1 tbs dry sherry
1 French bread stick
150ml (¼ pint) olive oil

To garnish
½ red pepper, deseeded and
  finely sliced
reserved pine kernels
4 sprigs of thyme

Stuffed Sugar Snaps

Can be made in advance
Preparation time: *20 minutes*
Cooking time: *5 minutes*

Makes 25

125g (4½oz) sugar snaps
110g (4oz) cream cheese
2 tbs chives, snipped
2 tbs parsley, finely chopped
110g (4oz) smoked salmon pâté
salt and freshly ground black pepper

This easy-to-make canapé lends itself to creative presentation. The sugar snaps can be stacked, lined in rows or even displayed on black lacquered oriental plates.

1   Using the point of a sharp knife, open each sugar snap by cutting along the curved edge.

2   Bring a small saucepan of water to the boil and immerse the sugar snaps for 1 minute to blanch. Remove immediately, drain, refresh under cold water and dry.

3   Mix the cream cheese, herbs, salt and freshly ground black pepper together.

4   Pipe the cheese mixture into half the sugar snaps, using a small pointed or serrated nozzle. Now fill the rest of the sugar snaps with the salmon pâté in the same way. Gently press the ends of the sugar snaps together.

5   To serve, arrange in alternate rows on a colour co-ordinated plate.

Oriental Chicken Filo Tarts

Can be made in advance
Preparation time: *20 minutes*
Cooking time: *15 minutes*

Photograph opposite page 60

These really mouth-watering little filo cups are filled with an oriental chicken mixture. You can prepare the filo tarts and the filling in advance, but only fill the tarts when ready to serve or they will go soggy.

1   Preheat the oven to 200°C (400°F/gas mark 6).

2   Using a 5cm (2in) round cutter cut the filo into circles.

3   Mix the olive oil with the beaten egg yolks. Brush each circle with the egg mixture and sit it in an oiled mini-canapé tin (the circles should be the same size as the tin). You will need 3 circle layers per cup.

4   Bake in the oven for about 10 minutes until golden brown.

5   Heat the sesame oil in a small frying pan or wok.

6   Add all the filling ingredients and stir fry for 5 minutes until the chicken is cooked.

7   To serve, fill the warmed tarts with the hot chicken mixture. Arrange in rows on a colourful plate – or on a black plate for a really dramatic effect. Garnish with the coriander leaves.

Makes 15

3 sheets filo pastry
2 tbs olive oil
2 egg yolks, beaten

Filling
1 boneless, skinless chicken breast, cut into very small pieces
2 tbs sesame oil
1 tbs soy sauce
3 spring onions, trimmed and finely chopped
1 clove of garlic, peeled and crushed
1 tsp ground coriander
1 tsp honey

To garnish
1 bunch coriander leaves

Apricot Sage and Mint Sausage Puffs

Can be made in advance
Will freeze
Preparation time: *15 minutes*
Cooking time: *20 minutes*

Makes *18 puffs*

375g (13oz) puff pastry
225g (8oz) sausage meat or
  minced lamb
1 egg, beaten
15g (½oz) each fresh sage
  and mint, stalks removed
55g (2oz) dried apricots
salt and freshly ground
  black pepper
2 egg yolks, beaten

These puffs are packed with distinctive flavours. Perfect for alfresco eating at your barbecue or picnic.

1 Preheat the oven to 220°C (425°F/gas mark 7).

2 On a lightly floured surface, roll out the puff pastry into a 12 x 35cm (4½ x 14in) rectangle.

3 Put all the other ingredients except the egg yolks into a food processor and process until well combined.

4 Spread the pastry with the meat filling, leaving a 1cm (½in) border all the way round the edge. Bring the edges together and pinch tightly, giving a curvy seal. Glaze the pastry with egg yolk then cut the puff into 18 slices.

5 Place the puffs on a baking tray lined with baking parchment and bake for 10–15 minutes until golden brown and crispy.

6 Serve hot or cold, or open-freeze when cooled.

Mexican Savoury Corn Cups

Can be made in advance
Will freeze (without fillings)
Preparation time: *20 minutes*
Cooking time: *20 minutes*

Tex-Mex here we come! These easy-to-make, irresistible, bite-sized savouries, with a selection of fillings, will set the scene for a spicy meal.

1 Preheat the oven to 180°C (350°F/gas mark 4).

2 Cream together the butter and cream cheese. Gradually add the flour, polenta, coriander, cayenne, water and salt to form a soft dough. Knead gently.

3 Take walnut-sized pieces of dough and roll into a ball. Press each ball down into small canapé tins, then ease the dough round the sides to form a cup.

4 Bake for 20 minutes or until golden.

5 Fill each cup with the fillings of your choice and serve immediately.

Makes 50

170g (6oz) butter, softened
85g (3oz) cream cheese
225g (8oz) plain flour
110g (4oz) fine polenta
1 tbs cold water
large bunch of coriander,
  chopped
pinch of cayenne pepper
pinch of salt

Suggested fillings
— guacamole
— chilli beans
— tomato salsa
— refried beans

Mozzarella and Spinach Choux Bites

Can be made in advance
Will freeze
Preparation time: *40 minutes*
Cooking time: *20 minutes*

***Makes** 40 bites*

125g (4oz) Mozzarella cheese
200ml (7fl oz) cold water
75g (3oz) butter
125g (4oz) plain flour
3 eggs, beaten
10 basil leaves, roughly torn
salt and freshly ground
  black pepper
225g (8oz) cooked spinach,
  chopped and drained well
125g (4oz) soft garlic
  cream cheese
1 large bunch basil, finely torn
2 tbs Parmesan cheese,
  grated (optional)

It is amazing how different choux pastry can taste when made with mozzarella cheese. They can be made larger and served as a starter.

1 Preheat the oven to 200°C(400°F/ Gas Mark 6)

2 Finely dice the mozzarella cheese.

3 To make the choux pastry, pour the water into a medium-sized saucepan. Add the butter to the water and melt over a low heat. Increase the heat and bring to a rolling boil.

4 Remove from the heat and immediately add all the flour. Beat to a smooth paste. Return to a low heat to dry a little, then cool until tepid. Add the eggs gradually, beating well between each addition. Now add the mozzarella and torn basil leaves and season well.

5 Place heaped tablespoons of the pastry onto a baking tray lined with damp baking parchment, leaving a space between each heap.

6 Bake for 15 minutes until puffed and golden. Leave to cool. Do not worry if the bites collapse at this stage as they will puff up when reheated.

7 To make the filling, mix the spinach, cream cheese and basil together until smooth. Season well.

8   To assemble the bites, make a slit in each choux bite
     and fill each bite with 1 tsp of filling. Place the bites
     back on to the lined baking tray. Sprinkle with
     Parmesan cheese, if using. Reheat in the oven for
     3–5 minutes.

9   To serve, stack the bites up on a plain plate or in a
     basket lined with cabbage leaves, radicchio or curly
     endive lettuce.

Smoked Trout Soufflé with a Fennel, Cucumber and Tomato Salad

Can be made in advance, if frozen raw
Will freeze
Suitable for Pesach
Preparation time: *20 minutes*
Cooking time: *20—25 minutes for small; 40—45 minutes for large*

Serves 8

175g (6oz) butter
4 tbs breadcrumbs, made from
  2 slices of bread (use medium
  matzo meal for Pesach)
55g (2oz) plain flour
  (substitute potato flour for
  Pesach)
300ml (10fl oz) milk
125g (4½oz) smoked trout
  fillets, skinned
2 tbs double cream or
  cream cheese
5 egg yolks, beaten
55g (2oz) fresh dill
pinch of nutmeg
6 egg whites
salt and freshly ground
  black pepper

Photograph between pages 60 and 61

This light and fluffy savoury soufflé never fails to impress. It is the party entertainer's dream as the raw mixture cooks perfectly from frozen – no mess, no noise – so you, too, can enjoy a drink with your guests.

1 Use 80g (3oz) of the butter to grease the sides and bottoms of 4 ramekin dishes or a 23cm (9in) soufflé dish. Coat the dishes with breadcrumbs, shaking out any excess. Use baking parchment to make a collar and secure around the outside of each dish with string or an elastic band (it will looks a little like a chef's hat).

2 Pre-heat the oven to 200°C (400°F/Gas Mark 6).

3 Make a white sauce by melting the rest of the butter in a small saucepan. Add the flour and cook for 1 minute over a low heat. Slowly add the milk, stirring continuously until thickened. Remove from the heat and set aside.

4 Place the trout with the cream or cream cheese in the food processor to make a purée.

5 Add the egg yolks, fish purée and dill into the white sauce in the food processor and whizz combine. Season with nutmeg, a little salt and plenty of freshly ground black pepper to the fish mixture.

6 Beat the egg whites until soft peaks are formed. Fold 1 tbs of beaten egg white into the fish mixture, using a metal spoon in a figure of eight movement. Add the remaining egg whites continuing to fold in lightly in the same way.

7 Pour the mixture into the prepared individual dishes or soufflé dish (you can freeze the soufflés at this point).

8 Bake individual soufflés for 25 minutes (35 minutes from frozen) or 45 minutes (1 hour from frozen) for the single dish.

9 While the soufflés are in the oven, make the salad. Mix together the fennel, cucumber and tomatoes. To make the dressing, whisk together the dill sauce, olive oil, dill and fennel fronds.

10 Arrange the fennel salad in a circle in the middle of the plate and drizzle over the dressing. Serve at once. When the soufflés are ready, loosen the sides with a sharp knife and invert into the centre of salad.

Salad
1 fennel bulb, finely chopped
½ cucumber, halved lengthways, deseeded and chopped
100g (4oz) cherry tomatoes, cut in to quarters
2 tbs Swedish dill sauce (omit for Pesach)
4 tbs extra virgin olive oil

To garnish
sprigs of dill and the fronds from the fennel

Trio of Salmon Risotto

Parev option
Preparation time: *10 minutes*
Cooking time: *30 minutes*

Serves *8–10 as a starter or*
4–6 as a main course

2 onions, peeled and finely
chopped
55g (2oz) butter
2 tbs olive oil
150ml (¼ pint) white wine
1.2 litres (2 pints) vegetable
stock
225g (8oz) Arborio or
Carniola rice
225g (8oz) fresh salmon,
skinned and cubed
3 tbs snipped chives
125g (4½ oz) smoked
salmon, cut into bite-sized
pieces
125g (4½oz) gravad lax, cut
into bite-sized pieces
3 tbs Parmesan cheese or
soya Parmesan for a meat
meal (optional)
salt and freshly ground
black pepper

Photograph between pages 60 and 61

This harmonious blend of flavours and textures produces a truly more-ish creamy risotto. It also makes a little salmon go a long way.

1 Using a deep frying pan, fry the onions in the butter and olive oil. Cook for a few minutes until softened.

2 In a separate saucepan, mix the white wine with the vegetable stock and heat until very hot.

3 Add the rice to the onions and continue to fry until the rice is translucent – this will take about 3 minutes.

4 Turn the heat to a low simmer and add one ladle of hot stock at a time to the rice. Continue to cook on a low simmer, gradually adding ladles of hot stock until the rice becomes just tender and most of the stock has been absorbed. Stir frequently to prevent the rice from sticking.

5 Add the fresh salmon and chives with the last ladle of stock, mix well and continue to cook until the salmon is cooked.

6 Remove from the heat and add the smoked salmon, gravad lax, Parmesan cheese or soya parmesan, if using, salt and freshly ground black pepper. Sprinkle with snipped chives and serve immediately.

To garnish
3 tbs snipped chives

Chicken Liver Caesar Salad

Can be made in advance (croutons and mayonnaise only)
Preparation time: *20 minutes*
Cooking time: *20 minutes*

Serves 4

Croutons

6 slices of bread (brown or
white), crusts removed and
cubed
3 tbs olive oil
2 tbs soya grated Parmesan
cheese (optional)
salt and freshly ground
black pepper

Caperberry mayonnaise

2 tsp caperberries or capers,
rinsed with stalks removed
1 egg
25g (1oz) caster sugar
1 tsp whole grain mustard
150ml (¼ pint) vegetable or
groundnut oil
salt and freshly ground
black pepper

Photograph between pages 60 and 61

This is a popular salad with a Jewish twist. Chicken livers can be prepared before hand up to the frying stage. The dish works equally well with cold or warm chicken livers. As an alternative use small strips of stir fried chicken-breast, salmon or tuna.

1 To make the croutons (can be prepared 1 day in advance), preheat the oven to 200°C (400°F/gas mark 6). Place the cubes of bread onto a baking tray lined with baking parchment. Drizzle with the olive oil. Season with salt and freshly ground black pepper and sprinkle with soya cheese, if using. Bake for 10 minutes (watch the croutons carefully as they have a very nasty habit of turning into cinders). Remove from the oven and cool on the baking tray. Set aside until ready to use.

2 Net, prepare the caperberry mayonnaise (can be done 2–3 days in advance and refrigerated), put the caperberries or capers, egg, sugar, mustard, salt and freshly ground black pepper into a food processor. Process together briefly. Slowly pour in the oil while the food processor is on, so a wonderful thick mayonnaise begins to form. If it becomes too thick, add a little more oil and a tablespoon of warm water to thin. Refrigerate until required.

3   To make the salad, cook the baby leeks and asparagus in simmering water until al dente. Refresh in cold water to maintain their colour and crispness. Drain and set aside. Split the little gem lettuces and cut the centre cores into 4 segments. Decorate the plate with a circular pattern of lettuce, asparagus and leeks. Scatter with dried cranberries or cherries, and caperberries or capers.

4   Dip the chicken livers in beaten egg and coat with seasoned flour or matzo meal. Heat up the oil in a large frying pan until very hot. Add the chicken livers and stir carefully for 3–4 minutes. Slice the chicken livers into small pieces. Add the red wine and cook for another 2 minutes until browned.

5   To serve, scatter the sliced chicken livers and croutons over the lettuce leaves, asparagus and leeks and spoon over a little caperberry mayonnaise.

Salad

170g (6oz) baby leeks, cut lengthways into 4
100g (4oz) baby asparagus or asparagus tips
4 little gem lettuces
4 tbs dried cranberries or cherries
4 tbs caperberries or capers, rinsed with stalks removed

Chicken livers

600g (1¼ lb) koshered chicken livers
1 large egg, beaten
4 tbs flour or medium matzo meal
3 tbs vegetable oil or groundnut oil
4 tbs red wine
salt and freshly ground black pepper

Individual Tomato Tarte Tatin

Can be made in advance
Parev option
Preparation time: *50 minutes, plus 30 minutes for the pastry to chill*
Cooking time: *1 hour*

Serves 6

Filling

35–40 large cherry
  tomatoes, halved
7 tbs olive oil
3 tbs balsamic vinegar
2 garlic cloves, peeled and
  finely chopped
225g (8oz) caster sugar
30 shallots, peeled
80g (3oz) grated Parmesan
  (soya Parmesan for parev
  option)

Pastry

300g (10½oz) plain flour
140g (5oz) butter or margarine
1 tbs fresh basil
½ tsp salt
2 egg yolks, beaten

Salad

6 tbs extra virgin olive oil
2 tbs balsamic vinegar
1 tsp caster sugar
mixed salad leaves

Photograph between pages 60 and 61

This is a good example of a starter that can be made in stages. You can roast the tomatoes, make the pastry, line the tins and fill with caramel and fry the shallots in advance. One large tart is quicker to make but may fall apart when cut into wedges so show your guests the whole tart before serving! Serve hot or cold with a mixed leaf salad.

1 Preheat the oven to 180°C (350°F/gas mark 4).

2 Place the tomato halves, cut side up, in a shallow roasting tin and drizzle 5 tbs olive oil and 3 tbs balsamic vinegar evenly over them. Sprinkle with garlic and season well. Bake for 10 minutes. Transfer the tomatoes on to absorbent paper and leave to drain.

3 Place all the pastry ingredients into the food processor and add 5–6 tbs water. Process until the dough forms a ball. Wrap in cling film, flatten and chill in the fridge for 30 minutes.

4 Line six individual shallow tart tins (do not use loose-bottomed tins) with baking parchment.

5 Dissolve the sugar in 6 tbs water in a small saucepan over a low heat. Bring to the boil and cook, without stirring, until caramel brown. Pour this immediately into each of the bases of the prepared tins and set aside.

6 Heat the remaining 2 tbs of olive oil in a frying pan. Fry the halved shallots over a medium to high heat until soft and browned.

7 Firmly pack the tomatoes, cut sides down, into each of the bases of the tins. Fill the gaps with shallots and sprinkle with Parmesan.

8 Roll the pastry out on a lightly floured surface. Use a 10cm (4in) pastry cutter to cut out 6 circles. Place over the tomatoes in the tin and seal the edges. Glaze with the beaten egg yolks.

9 Bake for 30 minutes or until the pastry is golden. Carefully drain off any excess liquid by tilting the dish slightly.

10 Invert each tarte onto a separate plate. Remove the baking parchment. Whisk together the olive oil, balsamic vinegar and sugar. Toss the mixed salad leaves in the dressing then use for garnish. Serve immediately.

Marinated Tuna with Balsamic Vinegar

Can be made in advance
Parev option
Suitable for Pesach
Preparation time: *20 minutes*
Cooking time: *No cooking required but needs overnight refrigeration*

Serves 6

12 very thin slices of fresh tuna

Marinade
150ml (¼ pint) extra virgin
*   olive oil*
1 bunch each of tarragon and
*   chives, chopped*
zest and juice of 1 lime
3 tbs white wine
salt and freshly ground
*   black pepper*

Dressing
200g (7oz) caster sugar
125ml (4fl oz) balsamic vinegar
3 bay leaves
3 sprigs rosemary
2 cloves garlic, peeled and
*   finely chopped*
juice of 1 lime
250ml (9fl oz) olive oil

To garnish
1 bunch of lamb's lettuce or a
*   bag of mixed salad leaves*
1 radicchio lettuce

Here raw tuna is marinated in herbs, giving the fish a wonderful flavour. This recipe works just as well with raw salmon.

1   Mix all the marinade ingredients together. Place the tuna in a bowl and pour over the marinade. Cover with clingfilm and leave to marinate in the fridge overnight. (The marinade will, in effect, 'cook' the tuna.)

2   To make the dressing, combine the sugar with 4 tbs water in a saucepan and stir over a low heat until dissolved. Bring to the boil and cook, without stirring, until caramel brown. Remove from the heat and very gradually add the vinegar (otherwise it will spit). Return to a low heat and stir until smooth. Remove from the heat and stir in the herbs, garlic, lime juice and olive oil. Leave to cool and strain before using.

3   To serve, place 2 slices of tuna onto a plate and decorate with the salad leaves. Drizzle the dressing over the whole dish.

Oriental chicken filo tarts (p. 47), mini stuffed potato skins (p. 39) and sushi (p. 41–43)

Smoked trout soufflé (p. 52-3)

Trio of salmon risotto (p. 54-5)

Chicken liver Caesar salad (p. 56-7)

Individual tomato tarte tatin (p. 58-9)

Spaghetti supper vegetable soup with rocket and basil pesto dressing (p. 76-7) accompanied by Italian bread with sun-dried tomatoes (p. 85)

Layered Mediterranean salmon fillet (p. 96–7) on a bed of sesame pak choy (p. 98)

Roasted vegetables in filo baskets with tomato and red pepper sauce (p. 99-100)

Penne and Parmesan Frittata

Can be made in advance
Preparation time: *25 minutes*
Cooking time: *50 minutes*

This is an impressive, tasty starter, which can be made in advance and reheated through gently when required. Served with a salad, it makes a delicious light lunch or supper. It is a creative way to use up leftover pasta.

1   Preheat the oven to 190°C (375°F/gas mark 5).

2   Cook the penne in salted boiling water until al dente.

3   While the pasta is cooking, heat the olive oil in a large frying pan. Fry the onions and pepper over a medium heat until softened. Add the cherry tomatoes and cook for a further 5 minutes. Leave to cool.

4   Combine the eggs, cheese, milk and herbs in a large bowl and whisk well. Stir in the tomato mixture and pasta and season to taste.

5   Line a 23cm (9in) spring-form baking tin with baking parchment and grease with a little oil. Spoon in the mixture. Bake for 40 minutes or until set.

6   Turn the frittata out onto a serving platter and remove the baking parchment. Cut into wedges and serve warm, garnished with large slices of parmesan, thyme and the ground black pepper.

Serves 6

200g (7oz) dried penne (pasta)
2 tbs olive oil
*2 onions, peeled and
   finely chopped*
*½ red pepper, deseeded and
   finely chopped*
*100g (3½ oz) cherry tomatoes,
   skinned and halved*
6 medium eggs
*110g (4oz) Parmesan
   cheese, grated*
120ml (4fl oz) milk
*3 tbs mixed herbs (such as
   thyme, chives, basil, sage),
   coarsely chopped*

To garnish
*8 slices of freshly shaved
   Parmesan cheese*
8 sprigs of thyme
*freshly ground
   black pepper*

Colourful Goat's Cheese Terrine Served with a Basil and Rocket Salad

Can be made in advance
Suitable for Pesach
Preparation time: *40 minutes*
Cooking time: *1 hour 40 minutes, plus 1 hour cooling time*

Serves 6–8

Terrine
*2 large each yellow and red
  peppers, quartered and
  deseeded
2 tbs olive oil
300g (10½oz) Desirée potatoes,
  peeled and thinly sliced
15g (½oz) butter
1 medium leek, washed and
  finely chopped
2 eggs
284ml (½ pint) sour cream
80g (3oz) soft goat's cheese
  (or similar for Pesach)
55g (2oz) fresh basil, torn*

Salad
*6 tsp extra virgin olive oil
4 tbs basil
1 tsp caster sugar
200g (7oz) rocket
150g (5oz) watercress
salt and freshly ground
  black pepper*

1 Preheat the oven to 180°C (350°F/gas mark 4).

2 Grease and line a 2lb loaf tin with baking parchment.

3 Brush the quartered peppers with olive oil and grill skin side up until the skin starters to blister. Immediately put the peppers into a bowl and cover with cling film.

4 Cook the sliced potatoes in boiling salted water until just tender. Drain and leave to cool.

5 Melt the butter in a small frying pan and sauté the leeks until softened. Leave to cool.

6 Combine the eggs, sour cream and goats' cheese and mix until smooth. Add the leeks and basil to the egg mixture, season well and mix. Spoon one third of the egg mixture into the loaf tin. Layer with potato, red pepper and half the remaining egg mixture. Repeat with the yellow pepper, potato and the remaining egg mixture

7 Cover tightly with greased tin foil and place the tin in a roasting tin. Pour in enough hot water to come half-way up the side of the loaf tin to make a bain marie. Bake for 1 hour and 10 minutes. Uncover and cook for a further 30 minutes. Remove the tin from the bain marie and allow to stand at room temperature for 1 hour.

8 Whisk together all the dressing ingredients. Turn out the terrine onto a serving platter, cut into slices and serve warm or cold on a bed of rocket and watercress. Drizzle the whole dish with the dressing and top with a leaf of both rocket and watercress.

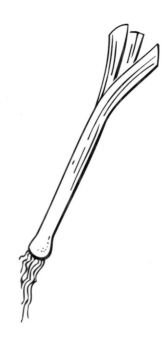

Brioche Stuffed with Wild Mushrooms

Can be made in advance
Will freeze (without the filling)
Preparation time: *40 minutes for brioche, plus 4 hours total rising time*
Cooking time: *20 minutes for brioche, 40 minutes for mushroom filling*

Makes 10

Brioche
2 sachets dried yeast
35ml (1¼ fl oz) warm milk
1 tsp salt
300g (10½oz) plain flour
3 medium eggs
175g (6oz) butter, softened
5g (¼oz) caster sugar
2 egg yolks, beaten
1 tbs milk

This makes an impressive starter and a good one to plan ahead and do in stages. It is well worth making time to bake your own brioche but the recipe works equally well with ready-made. Make double the quantity of the brioche so that you have some for another time.

1 Place the yeast, warm milk, salt, flour and eggs in a mixing bowl and beat. Beat the softened butter and sugar together and then gradually add to the first bowl.

2 Knead the dough with the dough hook of an electric mixer or by hand until it is smooth, shiny and elastic. Leave to rise in an oiled bowl, covered with oiled cling film in a warm place, near a radiator or in a warm kitchen for 1–1½ hours until doubled in bulk.

3 Knock back the dough by flipping over quickly with your finger tips not more than two or three times. Cover and place in the fridge for several hours or overnight.

4 Weigh out 55g (2oz) pieces of dough. Cut off one third of each to make the 'head'. Shape the larger piece into a ball and place into the greased mould (little brioche tins). Press a hole in the centre with a floured fingertip. Roll out the head into an

elongated egg shape, then gently press the narrow end into the hole in the centre of the large ball with lightly floured fingertips.

5 Preheat the oven to 220°C (425°F/gas mark 7).

6 Leave the dough to rise in a warm place for 20 minutes covered with oiled cling film. Glaze thoroughly with the egg yolks.

7 Place in the oven and bake for about 10–15 minutes until golden brown. Take in out of the mould immediately and leave to cool.

8 To make the filling, heat the oil in a large frying pan. Fry the red onion and garlic until softened. Add the mushrooms and continue to fry until softened. Add the red wine and cream. Increase the heat to reduce some excess liquid and also to cook off the raw alcohol taste. Season well with salt and pepper.

9 Before assembling the brioche, first preheat the oven to 180°C (350°F/gas mark 4).

10 Remove the heads from each brioche. Scoop out the inside of the body of each brioche. Place the bodies and heads on a baking tray. Warm in the oven for 5 minutes. Spoon the hot mushroom mixture into each brioche. Replace the heads and serve immediately on warmed plates garnished with parsley.

Mushroom filling
3 tbs olive oil
1 red onion, peeled and finely chopped
4 garlic cloves, peeled and crushed
900g (2lb) wild mushrooms (a mixture of brown cap, oyster, shiitake, button, chanterelles, cèpes, girolles)
3 tbs red wine
300ml (½ pint) double cream
2 tbs truffle oil, white or black (optional)
salt and freshly ground black pepper

To garnish
1 bunch parsley, finely chopped

Haddock and Orange Terrine

Can be made in advance
Will freeze
Parev option
Suitable for Pesach (terrine only)
Preparation time: *30 minutes*
Cooking time: *40 minutes*

Serves 6

Terrine
225g (8oz) haddock
  (or cod if preferred),
  skinned, boned and cubed
1 tbs orange zest
2 tbs orange juice
2 tbs fresh dill
freshly ground black pepper
2 egg whites
150ml (¼ pint) whipping cream
  (or parev cream)
225g (8oz) smoked salmon

Salad
3 oranges
2 heads of chicory
2 tbsp dill

Dressing
3 tbs walnut oil
1 tbs raspberry vinegar
salt and freshly ground
  black pepper
1 tbs caster sugar

To garnish
dill sprigs

This speedy combination of refreshing flavours speckled with pink smoked salmon makes a stylish, tasty and colourful hors d'oeuvre. Can be served warm or cold.

1 Preheat the oven to 180°C (350°F/Gas Mark 4).

2 Place the fish in a food processor with the orange zest, orange juice, dill and plenty of pepper. Process until smooth. Chill covered in the freezer for 10 minutes.

3 Lightly oil a 900g (2lb) loaf tin terrine and line the base with baking parchment.

4 Put the chilled fish back in the processor and, with the machine running, add the egg whites through the feeder tube. Then add the cream – do not overwork or the mixture will curdle. Mix in the smoked salmon so the mixture is flecked with pink.

5 Carefully fill the terrine with the mixture, packing it down well. Cover the terrine with baking parchment. Stand it in a roasting tin and pour in enough hot water to come halfway up the side of the terrine to make a bain marie.

6 Bake in the oven for 35–40 minutes or until firm to the touch. Run a thin-bladed knife around the terrine and turn it out of the mould on to a chopping board.

7 Peel and segment the oranges, removing the pith and membrane. Cut the hard, stalk end off the chicory and separate the leaves. Chop the dill. Mix the salad ingredients together.

8 Whisk all the dressing ingredients together. Toss the salad with the dressing.

9 Cut the terrine into thick slices and arrange on individual plates. Garnish with dill and serve with the salad.

Smoked Goose Breast with Sugar Snap and Almond Salad

Can be made in advance
Preparation time: *15 minutes*
Cooking time: *none*

Serves 6

Dressing
Juice of 2 limes
2 tsp honey
75ml (2½fl oz) extra virgin
olive oil
2 tsp sesame oil
2 tsp soy sauce
3 spring onions, trimmed and
thinly sliced on the diagonal
2 sticks of celery, finely chopped
1 tsp fresh ginger, peeled
and grated

Salad
2 green apples, cored and
thinly sliced
1 bunch of watercress
1 mixed bag of salad
110g (4oz) sugar snaps,
thinly sliced
12 slices smoked goose breast
(use smoked chicken if
preferred)
55g (2oz) toasted slivered
almonds

This is everything a busy person requires for an exceptionally quick starter. The dressing can be made in advance and refrigerated for up to 2 days. This just leaves the salad to be arranged at the last minute. For a vegetarian alternative use your favourite kosher blue cheese.

1 First prepare the dressing by combining all the ingredients and mixing well.

2 To make the salad, toss the apple in some of the dressing. Decorate 6 individual dinner plates with the salad leaves, sugar snaps and apple. Drizzle over the dressing. Fan the goosebreast on top of the salad. Scatter with the toasted almonds and serve immediately.

5

Soups and Breads

Soup can be a light starter or a substantial meal — winter warming or cool and refreshing on a summer's day. Most of the soup recipes in this book can be prepared in advance to be reheated and served hot or chilled and served cold. The crucial element of the soup will be the quality of your stock. This must be well flavoured and put together with the finest and freshest vegetables, herbs, beans, spices, fish, chicken or meat.

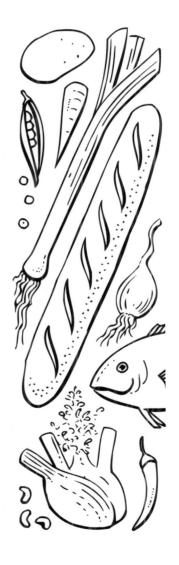

Soup variations are endless but the magic comes when you learn the art of combining flavours without letting one flavour overpower the others. The flavours should complement each other by blending or contrasting.

Take care over which soup you choose to make. For example, Spicy Mushroom and Lemon Grass Soup (see p.72) is perfect with an oriental main course. Avoid repeating the same ingredients throughout your meal. Furthermore, don't make a very filling soup if your main dish is a hearty one.

Making Soup

- When soups include fresh herbs or delicate vegetables such as watercress, these should be added just before the soup is puréed to preserve the flavour or colour.

- Don't purée every soup – leaving whole identifiable ingredients gives texture and allows the individual flavours to surface. Chop carrots and other vegetables into batons or flowers to enhance the final appearance.

- A stylish garnish can make an amazing difference to your soup. Choose from herbs, croutons, puff pastry shapes, oils, cream and spices for a final flourish. Keep your choice relevant and simple by linking the topping and the main ingredient. For example, an avocado gazpacho is finished with chopped avocado, tomato and pepper.

- Don't season your soup until the final stages – you need all the flavours developed to get it right.

- Seasoning and texture of soups will vary over time and with refrigeration and freezing. A soup made one day will taste different the next. Generally, soups with a blend of flavours improve with time whereas simple soups are best eaten immediately.

- Adding double cream and milk gives a soup a delicious velvety texture. The trick is to get the balance between vegetable and cream right to create the perfect soup.

- To thicken a soup, add rice, pasta or potatoes and cut down on the quantity of stock. This is far better than adding flour.

- When adding low-fat dairy liquids such as yoghurt to a soup, make sure that the soup is cool or it will curdle. Don't boil any soup containing low-fat dairy ingredients for the same reason.

- Undercooking or overcooking can ruin the final result. Delicately-flavoured soups should be undercooked. Meat soups or those with strong ingredients benefit from prolonged cooking to bring out the flavour – the longer the chicken soup simmers, the better the taste.

Spicy Mushroom and Lemon Grass Soup

Can be made in advance
Parev option
Suitable for Pesach
Preparation time: *30 minutes*
Cooking time: *25 minutes*

Serves 6

100g (4oz) dried mushrooms
2 stalks lemon grass
2 litres (3½ pints) vegetable stock
2 spring onions, trimmed and thinly sliced
2 shallots, peeled and finely sliced
450g (1lb) mushrooms, including black cap, oyster, wild mushrooms, sliced
1 small tin of wild mushrooms, drained and rinsed
4 large salad tomatoes, skinned and deseeded
2 small red chillies, deseeded and sliced
5 kaffir leaves (optional)
2.5cm (1in) ginger, finely chopped
2 garlic cloves, peeled and crushed
4 tbs lemon juice
1 tsp Chinese five spice
1 tbs light soy sauce

To garnish
coriander leaves

An aromatic taste of the Orient bursting with flavour!

1 Cover the dried mushrooms in boiling water and soak for 10 minutes.

2 Cut the lemon grass into 2.5cm (1in) lengths.

3 In a large saucepan, heat the stock with the lemon grass, spring onions and shallots. Bring to the boil and simmer for 2 minutes. Add all the mushrooms, including the soaking water. Cover and simmer for 5 minutes.

4 Stir in the tomatoes, chillies, kaffir leaves (if using), ginger, garlic, lemon juice, Chinese five spice and the soy sauce. Simmer for 10 minutes. Remove from the heat and discard the lemon grass.

5 Serve garnished with coriander leaves.

Mint and Chive Sweet Potato Vichyssoise

Can be made in advance
Will freeze
Parev option
Suitable for Pesach
Preparation time: *15 minutes*
Cooking time: *30 minutes*

This soup has a beautiful pale apricot colour, with a hint of green, and the consistency of single cream. It is traditionally served cold but may be heated gently if preferred.

1 Heat the olive oil in a large saucepan and gently sauté the prepared vegetables.

2 Add the vegetable stock and season well with the salt and freshly ground black pepper. Bring the soup to the boil and simmer for 25 minutes until the vegetables are soft.

3 Liquidize together with the fresh mint and chives. Leave to cool. Refrigerate until ready to serve.

4 Add the cream and check the seasoning just before serving. Although vichyssoise is traditionally served cold, this soup can be heated gently if preferred, but do not boil as the cream will curdle.

5 Serve garnished with chopped chives.

Serves 10-12

6 tbs olive oil
1.4kg (3lb sweet potatoes, peeled and roughly chopped
1.4 kg (3lb) leeks, washed, trimmed and roughly chopped
4 spring onions, trimmed and chopped
1 mild green chilli, deseeded and chopped
2 vegetable stock cubes, made up to 1.4 litres (2½ pints) of stock
2 tbs chopped mint
2 tbs chopped chives
425ml (¾ pint) single cream (use soya cream for parev option)
salt and freshly ground black pepper

To garnish
2 tbs chopped chives

73

Soupe de Poisson Served with French Bread, Gruyère and Rouille

Can be made in advance
Will freeze
Preparation time: *40 minutes*
Cooking time: *1 hour 10 minutes*

Serves 10–12

Vegetable stock

4 tbs extra virgin olive oil
2 red onions, peeled and
* chopped*
6 garlic cloves, peeled and
* chopped*
1 head celery, chopped
1 fennel, chopped
900g (2lb) tomatoes,
* cut into halves*
Pinch of saffron
5 juniper berries
3 star anise
10 black peppercorns
2 tsp salt
150ml (¼ pint) red wine
2 tbs sun-dried tomato paste

Soupe de poisson

6–10 bones and head from
* seabass, red mullet bream*
1 large leek, washed, trimmed
* and chopped*
6 garlic cloves, peeled
2 red onions, peeled and
* chopped*
2 carrots, peeled and chopped

Don't be put off by the number of ingredients — the method is simple and the result well worth it. This is a perfect example of a rustic restaurant dish that you can recreate for yourself. It will fill your kitchen with flavours of the Mediterranean!

1 First prepare the vegetable stock. In a large saucepan, sauté all of the vegetables in the olive oil for 10 minutes. Add enough water to cover. Add the saffron, juniper berries, star anise, peppercorns, salt, red wine and sun-dried tomato paste. Simmer for 20 minutes. Turn up the heat and simmer until the volume is reduce by a third (approximately 15 minutes).

2 Preheat the oven to 200°C (400°F/gas mark 6).

3 Place all of the soupe de poisson ingredients in a roasting tin, adding a little water to prevent the vegetables from burning. Roast for half an hour. Remove the roasting tin from the oven and add its contents to the hot stock.

4 Liquidise the soupe, including the bones, until smooth. Pass through a fine sieve, then liquidise the contents of the sieve to yield more soup. Strain this soup through a fine sieve and add to the first batch.

5 Place all the rouille ingredients, except the olive oil, into a food processor or liquidiser. Process to a thick paste. While the machine is running, slowly add the olive oil until a mayonnaise is made (this can be made in advance and kept for up to 3 days in the refrigerator).

6 To serve, put the rouille, bread and grated Gruyère into separate serving dishes. Heat the soupe and serve in individual warmed bowls. Your guests complete their soupe by putting a French bread slice into the soup bowl, adding some cheese and spooning in the rouille to taste.

1 bunch of thyme
1 glass red wine
salt and freshly ground
*   black pepper*
1 tsp paprika

Rouille
1 thick slice of bread
4 cloves garlic
pinch of saffron
2 medium egg yolks
juice of ½ lemon
salt
cayenne pepper
4 tbs of the soupe de poisson
touch of kosher Vermouth
*   (optional)*
1 tsp sundried tomato paste
150ml (¼ pint) olive oil

To garnish
1 stick of French bread, sliced
*   and lightly toasted*
225g (8oz) Gruyère, freshly
*   grated*

Spaghetti Supper Vegetable Soup with Rocket and Basil Pesto Dressing

Can be made in advance (soup only)
Will freeze (soup only)
Parev option
Preparation time: *20 minutes*
Cooking time: *45 minutes*

Serves 8

Soup

2 tbs olive oil
4 large potatoes, peeled and chopped
6 spring onions, trimmed and chopped
1 swede or turnip, peeled and chopped
1 large leek, trimmed and roughly chopped
2 cloves garlic, chopped
2.3 litres (3½ pints) vegetable stock
500ml (1pint) passata (sieved tomatoes)
200g (7oz) baby spinach, washed and chopped
100g (4oz) spaghetti
100g (4oz) frozen peas
4 plum tomatoes, peeled, deseeded and finely chopped
salt and freshly ground black pepper

Photograph between pages 60 and 61

Pasta with soup is a most successful partnership as the Italians have shown us over the years. This soup is a meal in itself, and makes an ideal winter warming supper or lunch. To make a really hearty meal serve it with chunky Italian bread. The pesto dressing adds the final flourish to one of my personal favourite soups.

1 Heat the olive oil in a large saucepan and sauté the potatoes, spring onions, swede or turnip, leek and garlic for 10 minutes until softened.

2 Add the stock and passata and bring to the boil. Simmer for 20 minutes or until the vegetables are soft.

3 Liquidise the vegetables until smooth and return to the saucepan. Season with lots of salt and freshly ground black pepper.

4 Sweat the chopped spinach in a covered dry pan until just soft. Drain well.

5 Cook the pasta following the instructions on the packet.

6 Place the frozen peas in a colander and pour boiling water over them to warm through.

7 To make the dressing, place all the ingredients, except the olive oil, in the liquidizer and blend until a thick paste. While the machine is running, gradually add the olive oil until the pesto is made. Check the seasoning. The pesto can be kept for up to 2 days in the refrigerator.

8 To serve, place a large spoonful of spaghetti at the bottom of each warmed soup bowl. Ladle in the soup followed by the peas, spinach and chopped tomatoes. Top with the pesto dressing.

Dressing
100g (4oz) rocket
1 clove garlic, peeled
25g (1oz) pine nuts, roasted in
*   a dry saucepan*
50g (2oz) Parmesan cheese
*   (omit for parev option)*
1 large bunch of basil
100ml (3½ fl oz) olive oil
salt and freshly ground
*   black pepper*

Ginger Spiced Parsnip and Lentil Soup

Can be made in advance
Will freeze
Parev option
Preparation time: *40 minutes*
Cooking time: *25 minutes*

Serves 6

3 tbs olive oil
5cm (2in) fresh ginger, peeled
and grated
225g (8oz) carrots, peeled and
chopped
225g (8oz) parsnips, peeled and
chopped
2 small onions or 4 spring
onions, peeled and chopped
2 leeks or 2 celery sticks,
washed, trimmed and chopped
1.4 litres (2½ pints) vegetable
stock
175g (6oz) red split lentils
200ml (7 fl oz) sour cream,
Greek yoghurt or crème
fraîche (omit for parev option)
1 tsp hot curry paste
salt and freshly ground black
pepper

To garnish
chopped celery leaves, parsley or
coriander

To serve
ciabatta or French bread

This hearty soup is marvellous as a warming lunch or supper if accompanied by French bread or ciabatta. Make the main broth in advance to develop the flavours.

1 Heat the olive oil in a large saucepan and sauté the ginger, carrots, parsnips, onions and leeks or celery until soft. Add the vegetable stock and lentils.

2 Simmer for 20–25 minutes until the vegetables and lentils are tender. You can prepare up to this stage in advance. Season to taste.

3 In a separate bowl, mix the sour cream, Greek yoghurt or crème fraîche with the curry paste.

4 Ladle the soup into warmed deep bowls and place a spoonful of the creamed curry paste on top. Garnish with celery leaves, coriander or parsley. Serve with chunks of French bread or ciabatta.

Summer Pea Soup

Can be made in advance
Will freeze
Parev option
Preparation time: *20 minutes*
Cooking time: *25 minutes*

This soup is ideal when fresh peas are cheap and plentiful. It is easy and quick to make and low in fat! For a winter pea soup, use frozen peas.

1 Heat the oil in a large deep saucepan and gently fry the spring onions until softened. Add the stock and stir in the mint and peas. Bring to the boil and simmer for 10 minutes. Add the lettuce, mangetout and seasoning. Simmer again for 5 minutes.

2 Purée half of the soup in a blender or food processor. Return the purée to the saucepan and mix well.

3 Serve piping hot, garnished with mint sprigs.

Serves 4-6

2 tbs vegetable oil
8 spring onions, trimmed and sliced
900ml (1½ pints) vegetable stock
2 tbs chopped mint
1kg (2lb) fresh peas in the pod or 500g (1lb) frozen petite pois, podded
½ green lettuce, shredded
110g (4oz) mangetout, trimmed and chopped
salt and freshly ground black pepper

To garnish
fresh sprigs of mint

Shredded Carrot and Celeriac Soup

Can be made in advance
Will freeze
Suitable for Pesach
Preparation time: *10 minutes*
Cooking time: *10 minutes*

Serves 6

3 tbs olive oil
3 shallots, peeled and
  finely chopped
4 cloves of garlic, peeled and
  finely chopped
6 medium carrots, peeled,
  grated or shredded in a
  food processor
1 medium celeriac, peeled,
  grated or shredded in a food
  processor
1.7 litres (3 pints) vegetable or
  chicken stock
3 slices of thick-cut smoked
  turkey, cut into matchsticks
225g (8oz) baby spinach,
  washed, stalks removed and
  chopped

This unusual, healthy meaty soup will soon become a regular favourite.

1 Heat the olive oil in a large saucepan.

2 Add the shallots and garlic and lightly fry.

3 Add the carrot, celeriac and stock. Simmer for 15-20 minutes.

4 Add the turkey and baby spinach. Cook for a further 5 minutes.

5 Serve at once or allow to cool before refrigerating or freezing.

Sherry Black Bean Soup

Can be made in advance
Will freeze
Parev option
Preparation time: *15 minutes*
Cooking time: *2½ hours, plus soaking beans overnight*

A hint of sherry permeates this chunky and striking bean soup.

1 Drain the beans, cover with fresh water, bring to the boil and continue to boil rapidly for 10 minutes. Drain and rinse them.

2 Heat the olive oil in a large saucepan and sauté the onion and garlic until softened but not coloured. Add the beans, stock, cumin seeds, oregano, bay leaves, cayenne and 2 tbs of the parsley. Bring to the boil and cover. Reduce the heat and simmer for 2 hours.

3 Stir in the red pepper, sherry, lemon juice, remaining parsley and brown sugar. Simmer for a further 10 minutes. Season to taste.

4 Serve hot in warmed bowls garnished with the lemon slices.

Serves 12

500g (1 lb) black beans, soaked in water overnight
2 tbs olive oil
2 large onions, peeled and finely chopped
8 garlic cloves, peeled and finely chopped
2 litres (3 ½ pints) chicken or vegetable stock
2 tbs cumin seeds
3 tbs fresh oregano, chopped
3 bay leaves, dried or fresh
pinch of cayenne pepper
4 tbs parsley, chopped
1 medium size red pepper, deseeded and finely chopped
200ml (7 fl oz) dry sherry juice of 2 lemons
1 tbs brown sugar
salt and freshly ground black pepper

To garnish
2 lemons cut into 12 thin slices

Roasted Butternut Squash and Smoked Cod Chowder

Can be made in advance
Will freeze
Parev option
Preparation time: *15 minutes*
Cooking time: *20 minutes*

Serves 6

900g (2lb) butternut squash,
 peeled and cut into 2 cms
 (1 in) cubes
4 tbs olive oil
3 garlic cloves, peeled and
 finely chopped
1 large onion, peeled and
 finely chopped
1.4 litres (2½ pints) vegetable
 stock
225g (8oz) smoked cod, skinned
 and cubed
2 x 330g (12oz) tins of
 sweetcorn
salt and freshly ground
 black pepper

To garnish
coriander leaves

This soup is really tasty and a little bit different from a normal chowder. To make life easier, roast the butternut squash the day before and refrigerate, then combine the other ingredients when you are ready to cook them. Vary the soup by using pumpkin when in season or adding different vegetables such as broad beans or a selection of wild mushrooms. If you prefer, smoked haddock is just as good.

1 Preheat the oven to 200°C (400°F/gas mark 6).

2 Place the cubed butternut squash in a roasting tin. Drizzle with 2tbs olive oil and sprinkle with chopped garlic. Season with salt and freshly ground black pepper. Roast for 20 minutes.

3 Sauté the onion in the remaining 2 tbs of olive oil until softened but not coloured. Add the hot vegetable stock, cod and sweetcorn. Bring to the boil. Add the roasted butternut squash and simmer for 15 minutes.

4 Ladle the soup into warmed bowls and garnish with coriander leaves.

Breads

Dried yeast

If you are using dried yeast, you will need half the quantity of fresh given in a recipe. This yeast needs to be reconstituted with a warm liquid before use. Liquid that is too hot will kill the yeast. Sugar is also needed to activate the yeast. You will know that the yeast is working when it starts to froth.

Fast action yeast

This is the most popular as it speeds up and simplifies bread-making. It does not need mixing with warm liquid and sugar to activate.

Kneading

This distributes the yeast and stretches the gluten. It will take about 3 minutes in an electric mixer (use a dough hook if available) and 5–10 minutes by hand. To knead by hand, place the dough on a lightly floured work surface. Using the heel of your hand, push down on the middle of the dough and stretch the top half away from you. Bring the top half back over to the middle. Make a quarter turn and repeat the stretching process. Keep turning and stretching for about 5–10 minutes. When ready, the dough will be smooth and spring back if prodded.

Rising

Bread dough needs to be left to rise until doubled in size. If the dough is left too long it will crack or have an over stretched appearance when it is baked. Where you leave the dough to rise influences how long the rising will take.

1-1½ hours	warm airing-cupboard or warm kitchen
1½-2 hours	room temperature
4 hours	cool place such as larder
2 hours-overnight	in the refrigerator

Knocking back

This is done after the dough has risen. Using your hands, firmly push the puffy risen dough back to its original size.

Shaping

Make the bread into different shapes and sizes. To make rolls, weigh out 75g (3oz) portions. This also ensures even batch cooking.

Proving

This is the second rising. The knocked-back, shaped dough is covered with oiled cling film and left to rise again in a warm place until doubled in size. This takes about 15 minutes for small rolls and 30 minutes for large loaves.

Glazes

Different glazes and toppings will give your breads interesting finishes and textures. Water will give a crisp crust, milk will give a pale colour, egg will give a golden colour and melted butter will give a softer crust. Sesame seeds, cumin seeds, coriander seeds, sunflower seeds, nuts, caraway, and poppy seeds are some of the sprinkles you could try.

Baking

Bread needs to be baked at 200–220°C (400–425°F/gas mark 6–7). The general rule is that the plainer the dough, the hotter the oven. To create a really crispy crust place a tray of boiling water in the oven. To test if the bread is cooked, tap the base. Bread is ready when it sounds hollow and light when tapped. Cool loaves and rolls on a cooling rack.

Freezing

All bread can be frozen once it has cooled.

Bread with Sun-dried Tomatoes

Can be made in advance
Will freeze
Parev option
Preparation time: *10 minutes, plus 1½ hours rising time, depending on the bread size*
Cooking time: *25–45 minutes*

Photograph between pages 60 and 61

This bread has a great red colour and makes excellent croutons if any is left after 3 days. Add 2 tbs of chopped fresh basil and/or 50g (2oz) black olives into the basic dough for a truly Italian combination!

Makes *1 loaf or 12 rolls*

500g (1 lb) strong white flour
2 tsp salt
7g (¼oz) dried yeast (1 sachet)
2 tbs extra virgin olive oil
2 tbs sun-dried tomatoes soaked in olive oil, finely chopped
425ml (¾ pint) warm water
1–2 egg yolks for glazing

1 Sift the flour and salt into a large mixing bowl. Add the yeast, extra virgin olive oil, sun-dried tomatoes and the water. Mix well until a firm dough has formed. Place the dough in an oiled bowl, cover and leave to rise for about 1½ hours in a warm place.

2 Preheat the oven to 230°C (450°F/gas mark 8).

3 Knock back the dough and either knead into a loaf shape or make into individual bread rolls.

4 For rolls, measure out 75g (3oz) pieces of dough and then shape. Place on to a baking tray lined with baking parchment and then glaze with egg yolk.

5 For a loaf, grease and line a loaf tin. Place the dough inside and glaze with the egg yolk. Leave to prove for 10 minutes for the rolls and 20 minutes for the loaf.

6 Place in the oven and bake for 10 minutes. Reduce the heat to 200°C (400°F/gas mark 6) and bake the loaf for 45 minutes and the rolls for 20–25 minutes until golden brown. Remove from the oven and place on a cooling rack.

Wild Mushroom Rolls

Can be made in advance
Will freeze
Parev option
Preparation time: *10 minutes, plus 1½ hours rising time depending on the bread size*
Cooking time: *15—45 minutes*

Makes *12 rolls or 2 loaves*

500g (1 lb) strong white flour
250g (9oz) multi-grain strong flour
2 tsp salt
1 tsp caster sugar
7g (¼oz) dried yeast (1 sachet)
2 tbs extra virgin olive oil
285g (9½oz) tin of mushroom or mushroom paste
75g (3oz) pine nuts
425ml (¾ pint) warm water
2 egg yolks

This savoury bread, which combines both multigrain and plain strong flour with mushrooms and pine nuts, is great with most starters and soup.

1 Place both flours, salt, sugar and yeast in a large mixing bowl. Add the oil, mushrooms and pine nuts. Gradually add water until you have a firm but not too sticky dough.

2 Grease a bowl with the olive oil, add the dough and cover with cling film. Leave to rise for 1–1½ hours.

3 Grease the loaf tins or baking sheet with a little vegetable oil and line with baking parchment.

4 Preheat the oven to 200°C (400°F/gas mark 6).

5 Knock back the dough and either knead into a loaf shape or make into individual bread rolls. If making individual rolls weigh up the dough into 75g (3oz) pieces. Glaze with egg yolk and leave to prove for 10 minutes.

6 Bake the individual rolls for 15–20 minutes and the large loaves for 45 minutes until golden brown.

Rosemary Ciabatta

Can be made in advance
Will freeze
Parev option
Preparation time: *10 minutes, plus 1½ hours rising time*
Cooking time: *20 minutes*

This fragrant combination of rosemary and olive oil will bring the true taste of Italy into your kitchen.

1 Mix together the yeast, salt and flour. Add the maple syrup or honey, oil and one third of the chopped rosemary until well combined. The mixture should be soft and shiny. Mix together slowly by hand or using a food mixer.

2 Gradually add the warm water until combined (you may not need to use all the water). Transfer into an oiled bowl, cover and leave to rise in a warm place for 1½ hours or until doubled in size.

3 Preheat the oven to 220°C (425°F/gas mark 7).

4 Knock back the dough. Divide the dough into 75g (3oz) pieces. Knead and then flatten each roll.

5 Place on a baking tray lined with baking parchment. Make thumb indentations and then drizzle with olive oil, sprinkle with sea salt and the remaining chopped rosemary leaves. Leave to prove for 10 minutes.

6 Bake the bread on the middle shelf for 20 minutes or until golden brown.

Makes 15 rolls

7g (¼oz) dried yeast (1 sachet)
2 tsp salt
750g (1½ lb) strong
  white flour
1 tbs maple syrup or
  clear honey
150ml (¼ pint) extra virgin
  olive oil, plus extra for
  drizzling
30g (1oz) fresh rosemary,
  finely chopped
425ml (¾ pint) warm water
sea salt

Crusty Cumin and Corn Bread

Can be made in advance
Will freeze
Parev option
Preparation time: *30 minutes, plus 1½ hours rising time*
Cooking time: *55 minutes*

Makes *2 loaves*

425ml (¾ pint) water
125g (4½oz) ground polenta
2 tbs olive oil
1 tbs cumin seeds, dry roasted
5g (¼oz) sea salt
14g (1½oz) dried yeast
  (2 sachets)
200g (7oz) cooked corn kernels,
  fresh, frozen or tinned
600g (1lb 5oz) flour, plus extra
  for dusting

This is a really tasty, crusty bread and complements perfectly spicy dishes such as Chicken Masala (see p.153–154). A dough hook on an electric mixer is an essential tool to get the right consistency.

1 Bring 425ml (¾ pint) of water to boil in a saucepan. Add the polenta in a steady stream, stirring constantly with a whisk. Continue to stir over a medium heat for 30–60 seconds until the polenta forms a mass and leaves the side of the pan. Take off the heat, stir in the olive oil, cumin seeds and salt. Leave to cool.

2 In a large mixing bowl, dissolve the yeast in 2½ tsp warm water. Add the polenta mixture and corn and beat with an electric mixer, using the dough hook if you have one, until well combined. Gradually add the strong flour and leave to mix for 10 minutes until it becomes smooth and elastic.

3 Flour your hands, as the dough will still be a little sticky and make a ball. Place in an oiled bowl, cover with cling film and leave to rise in a warm place for about 1½ hours until the dough has doubled in size.

4 Line a baking tray with baking parchment and sprinkle over the extra polenta.

5   Knock back the dough and cut in half.

6   Preheat the oven to 220°C (425°F/gas mark 7).

7   Sprinkle flour on to a flat surface and knead the dough into 2 round loaves about 15–18cm (6–7 in) in diameter. Cover with oiled cling film and leave to rise again for 40 minutes on a prepared tray. Remove the cling film.

8   Make 3 slits in the top of the dough with a sharp knife or a pair of scissors. Glaze the bread with egg yolk. Place in the preheated oven with a second tray underneath which has been half filled with boiling water (this is to give off steam during the cooking to make the bread really crispy).

9   Bake the bread in the middle shelf for 50–55 minutes or until golden brown. The bread is cooked if it sounds hollow when tapped on the base. Leave to cool on a wire rack.

Walnut, Apricot and Raisin Bread

Can be made in advance
Will freeze
Parev option
Preparation time: *45 minutes, plus 10 minutes rising time*
Cooking time: *15–20 minutes rolls; 30 minutes loaves*

Makes *6 mini loaves or*
  12 rolls

30g (1oz) dried yeast
  (2 sachets)
50ml (2fl oz) olive oil
50ml (2fl oz) walnut oil
1 kg (2¼ lb) strong plain flour
30g (1oz) salt
75g (3oz) chopped walnuts
55g (2oz) dried apricots,
  chopped
55g (2oz) raisins
570ml (1 pint) warm water
2 egg yolks

This is delicious served cold or warm with a starter or for a buffet or picnic. It goes particularly well with mature Cheddar cheese and grapes.

1 Place the yeast, both oils, flour and salt into a mixing bowl. Mix well.

2 Add the walnuts, apricots, raisins and warm water. Knead by hand for 10 minutes or 2 minutes using a mixer. Place in an oiled bowl, cover with cling film and leave to rise in a warm place for 45 minutes or until doubled in size.

3 Pre-heat the oven 220°C (425°F/gas Mark 7).

4 Knock back and then weigh out 6 x 300g (11oz) pieces for mini-loaves or 12 x 150g (5½oz) pieces for rolls.

5 Shape as desired and place on a baking tray lined with baking parchment. Glaze with egg yolk and leave to prove for 10 minutesfor the mini-loaves and 5 minutes for the individual rolls.

6 Bake the bread on the middle shelf for 15–20 minutes for the rolls or 30 minutes for the mini-loaves until golden brown.

6

Family and Festive Meals

Jewish celebrations often involve large gatherings of family and friends and the recipes in this chapter are intended to appeal to a broad range of tastes and ages. I have also tried to minimise the time you spend in the kitchen and maximise the amount of advanced preparation you can do. I have given new flavours and twists to the traditionally festive foods, salmon, chicken and lamb. My accompaniments use easily available but often ignored vegetables. By being adventurous but still staying within sight of traditional Jewish expectations, I hope to have refreshed your family and festive meal repertoire.

Best Ever Fish Pie

Can be made in advance
Will freeze
Pesach friendly
Preparation time: *40 minutes*
Cooking time: *1 hour 10 minutes*

Serves : 10

For the Fish Pie
*225g (8ozs) smoked cod
    Skinned and cubed*
*225g (8ozs) cod Skinned and
    cubed*
*225g (8ozs) smoked haddock
    skinned and cubed*
*225g (8oz) haddock
    skinned and cubed*
290ml (½ pint) milk
*225g (8ozs) peas
    (Use mushrooms for Pesach)*
*3 hard-boiled eggs
    shelled and chopped*
3 tbs chopped parsley

This is a real family favourite. It freezes well and I suggest that you make a large quantity as you will definitely be asked for seconds! You can vary the fish to your taste but I feel that the combination of both smoked and unsmoked gives the best flavour.

To make the Fish Pie

1   Pre-heat the oven to 200°C (400°F/gas mark 6).

2   Poach the fish by placing it all into a large ovenproof dish. Pour over the milk and cover. Cook for 20 minutes.

3   Drain the milk into a jug and make up to 290ml (½ pint) with extra milk, if necessary for the sauce.

4   Transfer the fish to a large and deep oven-to-table serving dish.

5   Cook the peas.

To make the Sauce

1 Melt all the butter in a large saucepan and fry the onions until they are softened but not coloured.

2 Add the cumin, coriander and curry powder and cook for 1 minute. This helps to bring out their true flavour.

3 Add the flour.

4 Cook this together for 1 minute.

5 Slowly add the milk and cream, stirring continuously until the mixture is of a thin custard consistency.

6 Season well with salt and freshly ground black pepper.

7 Pour the sauce over the fish.

8 Mix in the peas, chopped egg and parsley. (You can make it up to this stage a day in advance. Can be put in the fridge or frozen).

To make the Mashed Potato

1 Cook the potatoes until they are soft, and then mash them.

3 Add the butter, cream and seasoning and mix well.

4 Pipe or fork the mashed potato onto the top of the fish mixture. (If you have not already frozen the pie, you can freeze it at this point).

5 Cook for 35 minutes at 180°C (350°F/gas mark 4) until the fish mixture has warmed and the topping is golden and crispy. Serve immediately with a mixed leaf salad.

(This can be refrigerated for up to 2 days subject to freshness of the fish and the sell by dates for the milk, cream and eggs).

For the Sauce
140g (5oz) unsalted butter
3 onions peeled and
    finely sliced
1 tbs ground cumin
2 tbs ground coriander
2 tbs medium – mild curry
    powder
    (omit for Pesach)
50g (2ozs) plain flour
290ml (½ pint) double cream

For the Potato Topping
6–8 large potatoes
    peeled and cut into quarters
110g (4oz) unsalted butter
2 tbs double cream
salt and freshly ground
    black pepper
nutmeg

Fillet of Cod with Squash Purée and Tomato and Caper Sauce

Preparation time: *15 minutes*
Cooking time: *30 minutes*

Serves 4

4 tbs olive oil
2 garlic cloves, finely peeled
  and chopped
675g (1½ lb) butternut squash,
  peeled and chopped
2 tbs fresh sage, chopped
55g (2oz) unsalted butter or
  margarine
4 x 140g (5oz) cod fillets,
  skinned
salt and freshly ground
  black pepper

Sauce
Juice of half a lemon
1 tbs balsamic vinegar
2 tbs capers, rinsed
  (omit for Pesach)
2 ripe tomatoes, skinned,
  seeded and finely diced
1 tbs flat leaf parsley,
  finely chopped

To garnish
sugar snap peas (use asparagus
  for a Pesach option), cooked
4 sprigs parsley

Cod can be quite unexciting, but the squash purée and tomato and caper dressing give the dish life through colour, texture and flavour. If the cod is partly fried up to 4 hours ahead, it can be completed in the oven 10 minutes before you plan to serve it. This dish is quick to prepare, low in fat and children will love the sweetness of the squash.

1 Heat the 2 tbs of the olive oil in a heavy-based saucepan and sauté the garlic for 3 minutes until golden. Add the squash and sage and stir fry for 1–2 minutes. Add 4 tbs of water and simmer gently for 30 minutes until the squash is cooked.

2 Mash the squash until very smooth, beating in a little extra olive oil and salt and freshly ground black pepper. Cover and keep warm, or refrigerate and reheat when required. The mashed squash will keep up to 2 days the refrigerator.

3 Preheat the oven to 190°C (375°F/Gas Mark 5).

4 Melt the butter and the rest of the olive oil in a frying pan or griddle until golden brown and foaming. Add the cod, skin side down and fry for 2–3 minutes, until crisp and browned. (Butter tends to burn easily and the addition of oil prevents this. If the fat in the pan becomes burnt, wipe the pan clean

before starting to fry again.) Turn the fillets over and fry for a further 2–3 minutes.

5 Transfer the fish to an oven-proof dish. Season and sprinkle with lemon juice, balsamic vinegar, capers and tomatoes. Cover and bake in the oven for 5 minutes.

6 To serve, spoon the mashed squash onto 4 plates. Sit a fillet of cod on top of each mound with a little of the sauce. Arrange the cooked sugar snaps around the plate and add a sprig of parsley.

Layered Mediterranean Salmon Fillet

Can be made in advance
Parev option
Pesach friendly
Preparation time: *40 minutes*
Cooking time: *40 minutes*

Serves *8*

2kg (4½ lb) whole salmon,
  skinned and cut into two
  fillets
2 red and yellow peppers, each
  cut into quarters and
  deseeded
6 tbs olive oil
50g (2oz) dried aubergines or
  1 large fresh aubergine, sliced
  lengthways
2 tbs black olive tapenade (omit
  or make your own for Pesach
50g (2oz) fresh basil
2 tbs extra virgin olive oil
salt and freshly ground black
  pepper

To serve
baby new potatoes

Photograph between pages 60 and 61

This is a splendid centre piece for a special occasion. You will love the aubergine, basil and pepper combination within the salmon fillet. Once the peppers are skinned, they can be stored in a refrigerator up to 2 days in advance, and the rest of the preparation can be done in about 10 minutes. It is great for Seder night as it can be served hot or cold.

1 Cut the peppers in half and place on a baking tray skin side up. Brush the skins with 3 tbs olive oil. Place under a hot grill until the skins start to blister. Transfer the peppers to a bowl with a fork, and cover with cling film. Once the peppers have cooled, remove the skin. Refrigerate until ready to use.

2 Brush the aubergine slices with 3 tbs of olive oil and grill until soft.

3 Preheat the oven to 180°C (350°F/gas mark 4).

4 Cover a large baking tray with a large piece of baking parchment, allowing enough overlap to parcel the salmon stack. Place a salmon fillet, skinned side down on the tray. Spread with 1 tbs tapenade.

5 Layer with half the aubergine slices, salt and freshly ground black pepper, half the chopped basil leaves and all the red peppers. Continue layering with the remaining aubergine slices and basil and all the yellow peppers.

6 Spread the unskinned side of the second salmon fillet with the remaining tapenade. Place the salmon fillet on top of the stack, tapenade side down. Drizzle with the extra virgin olive oil and season the top of the salmon fillet with salt and freshly ground black pepper.

7 Make a parcel of up the stack with the baking parchment. Using three lengths of string, secure the parcel at intervals with knots. Refrigerate for up to 12 hours until ready to cook.

8 Bake for 35–40 minutes.

9 Serve with boiled baby new potatoes and Sesame Pak Choy (see p.98).

Sesame Pak Choy

Preparation time: *10 minutes*
Cooking time: *5–10 minutes*

Serves 8

3 tbs roasted sesame oil
4 tbs soy sauce
6–8 bunches pak choy
  (depending upon the size),
  shredded
2 tbs sesame seeds

Photograph between pages 60 and 61

Pak choy is Chinese cabbage. There are other types such as baby pak choy and choy sum. The only difference is their shape and colour. If none of these are available, use curly kale, greens or spinach instead.

1 Heat a wok with sesame oil and soy sauce.

2 Add the pak choy and sesame seeds, and cook until it has just began to wilt. Serve immediately.

Roasted Vegetables in Filo Baskets with Tomato and Red Pepper Sauce

Can be made in advance
Can be Parev
Preparation time: *30 minutes*
Cooking time: *25 minutes*

Photograph opposite page 61

This medley of bright colours and mixed flavours is delightful. It can all be made in advance in stages. Filo pastry varies in size, according to the manufacturer. Personally, I prefer fresh and not frozen as it is less likely to fall apart. The sauce is also ideal for pasta, chicken or even as part of a stew or soup.

To Make the Filo Baskets

1 Pre-heat the oven to 2000C (4000F/gas mark 6). Melt the butter.

2 Cut out 14.5 cms (6 inch) squares of filo so that you have 6 squares for each basket.

3 Prepare six ramekins by brushing the inside with melted butter. Place one square of filo on bakewell paper and brush with melted butter. Place a second square over this at an angle, creating a star shape. Brush again with melted butter. Repeat this until all 6 squares are used and the final square is buttered. Place inside the prepared ramekin, easing it in. Repeat the entire process until all six ramekins are lined with filo.

4 Line the inside of the filo baskets (still in the ramekins) with foil and pour in some baking beans. Bake for 10-15 minutes until golden and crispy. Remove the foil and beans immediately. Remove the

Serves 6

For the Filo Baskets

3 sheets of filo per basket
  Cut into half
225g (8oz) unsalted butter (or margarine + 3 tbs vegetable oil)

Parev option

For the Vegetables
2 medium green courgettes
  Cut into batons 2cm (1 in) lengths.
2 medium yellow courgettes (if available) Cut into batons 2cm (1in) lengths.
1 red pepper De-seeded and cut into large cubes
1 yellow pepper De-seeded and cut into large cubes
225g (8oz) baby leeks
  Trimmed and chopped
225g (8oz) asparagus spears
  Cut into 2cm (1in) lengths but keep the spear end intact

225g (8oz) wild mushrooms eg:
shiitake, oyster, brown cap or
a mixture of what is
available, cut into thick slices
4 garlic cloves, peeled and finely
chopped
5-6 tbs olive oil

baskets from the ramekins while they are warm as it is easier to lift out before the butter solidifies. (These can be made up to 1 day in advance and kept in an airtight container).

To make the Roasted Vegetables

1 Pre-heat the oven to 1800C (3500F/gas mark 4).
2 Put the prepared vegetables in a roasting tin.
3 Drizzle the olive oil over them, sprinkle with chopped garlic and season well. (This can be prepared up to 4 hours prior to roasting). Roast in the pre-heated oven for 20 minutes.

To make the Sauce

1 Pre-heat the oven to 1800C (3500F/gas mark 4).
2 Place the prepared red pepper and tomatoes in a roasting tin. Sprinkle with olive oil and salt and freshly ground black pepper. Roast in the pre-heated oven for 20 minutes.
3 Remove from the oven and place the entire contents into a food processor or liquidiser and process until smooth. Sieve. Re-heat before use. (This can be made in advance and stored in the refrigerator. Re-heat either in the microwave or gently in a saucepan. It will last 2-3 days).

To Serve

1 Reheat the filo baskets for 5-10 minutes in a pre-heated oven at 2000C (4000F/gas mark 6). Do not reheat in the microwave as this makes the pastry soggy!
2 Gently reheat the sauce and remove the hot and freshly cooked vegetables from the oven. Spoon the sauce onto the centre of each dinner plate and carefully sit a basket on top. Fill with the cooked vegetables. Some baby roast potatoes, a jacket potato or spaghetti with olive oil, chopped basil, salt and freshly ground black pepper is all that is needed to complete this dish.

Peanut and Tofu Vegetable Stir Fry with Crispy Noodles

Parev option
Preparation time: *30 minutes*
Cooking time: *15 minutes*

This parev dish is ideal for any vegetarian guest if you are serving meat. It is so tasty that even diehard meat lovers will want some!

1 Heat 4 tbs of the sesame oil in a large wok or frying pan.

2 Stir fry the tofu, ginger, garlic, red onion, red pepper, patty pans and tomatoes for 5 minutes. Add the hot vegetable stock. Stir and simmer for 1 minute.

3 Mix together all the sauce ingredients and add to the wok.

4 Continue to stir fry the vegetables until they are just cooked and evenly coated with peanut glaze. This will take another 3–5 minutes. Add the spinach and cook for a further 2 minutes. Put the vegetables onto a large warmed serving platter and cover to keep hot.

5 Add the remaining sesame oil to the wok and stir fry the noodles until crispy. Arrange the noodles around the vegetables. Scatter with the roasted cashew nuts, lime zest and chopped coriander.

Serves 6

7 tbs toasted sesame oil
200g (7oz) tofu of your choice, cut into 2cm (1in) pieces
5 cm (2in) fresh ginger, peeled and finely chopped
2 garlic cloves, peeled and crushed
2 red onions, peeled and sliced
2 red peppers, sliced into strips
100g (4oz) green and yellow patty pans, cut in half, or courgettes, cut in batons
100g (4oz) baby plum tomatoes, cut in half
2 tbs hot vegetable stock
250g (9oz) fine egg noodles, cooked
225g (8oz) baby spinach leaves, roughly chopped

Sauce

1 tbs clear honey
3 tbs satay sauce or peanut sauce
1 tbs hoisin sauce
1 tbs crunchy peanut butter
1 lime

To garnish

55g (2oz) roasted cashew nuts, chopped
1 bunch of fresh coriander

Turkey, Cranberry and Chestnut Pie with Cranberry Sauce

Can be made in advance
Will freeze
Preparation time: *35 minutes, plus 1 hour to chill the pastry*
Cooking time: *2 hours*

Serves 8

Pastry
450g (1lb) plain flour, plus
  extra for dusting
1tbs salt
2 eggs, beaten
65g (2½oz) margarine, plus
  extra for greasing
65g (2½oz) vegetable lard
200ml (7fl oz) water
beaten egg

Filling
3 tbs vegetable oil
2 large onions, peeled and
  finely chopped
700g (1½lb) turkey, cubed
450g (1lb) mixed mushrooms
  (such as oyster, button, brown
  cap), sliced
30g (1oz) mixed dried
  mushrooms, soaked in
  boiling water
1 large jar cranberry sauce
4 tbs chopped parsley

This big pie satisfies hearty eaters. It is a different way to present traditional winter ingredients. Take it whole to the table for it to be truly appreciated and admired. For a vegetarian variation, omit the turkey and use 700g (1½ lb) pumpkin, butternut squash or sweet potato that have been cooked until just soft.

1 First prepare the pastry. Sift the flour and salt into a mixing bowl. Make a well in the middle. Pour in the beaten eggs and cover with flour.

2 Put the water, margarine and lard into a small pan and melt over a moderate heat. Increase the heat and when boiling, pour onto the flour mixture, beating constantly with a wooden spoon until a ball is formed.

3 Turn the dough out onto a floured board. Knead until smooth. Wrap in cling film. Chill for about 1 hour until it is firm to the touch.

4 Make the filling while the dough is resting. Heat the oil in a large frying pan. Fry the onions and turkey for 10 minutes. Add the fresh mushrooms and the drained re-hydrated dried mushrooms. Continue to cook for 15–20 minutes until the turkey is cooked. Add the parsley, chestnuts and cranberry sauce with the turkey mixture and mix well.

5 Preheat the oven to 180°C (375°F/gas mark 6).

6 Cut off one third of the pastry and put to one side.

7 Roll the remaining pastry to fit a 23cm (9in) loose-bottomed deep pie dish, allowing fit to overhang the edge by 2.5cm (1in). Fill with the turkey mixture. Dampen the edges of the pastry with water.

8 Roll out the rest of the pastry to make the lid. Use any trimmings to make shapes to decorate the top. Crimp sides and neaten edges. Glaze with egg yolk.

9 Place the pie on to a heated oven tray, cover the top with foil to prevent burning and put in the oven. After 1 hour, remove the foil.

10 Raise the oven temperature to 200°C (400°F/gas mark 5). Loosen the sides of the pie dish. Glaze the pie sides with beaten egg yolk. Return the pie to the oven for the final 30 minutes, until it is golden.

11 To make the cranberry sauce, place all the ingredients in a saucepan and mix well. Boil until well combined and reduced by half. Check the seasoning.

12 Serve slices of pie with a little of the cranberry sauce, and Brussel Sprouts and Savoy Cabbage Stir Fry (see p.104).

2 x 200g (7oz) tins whole chestnuts or vacuum-packed dried, peeled chestnuts

Sauce
175g (6oz) fresh, frozen or dried cranberries
zest and juice of 1 orange
small jar of cranberry sauce
2 tbs kiddush wine

Brussel Sprouts and Savoy Cabbage Stir Fry

Preparation time: *10 minutes*
Cooking time: *10 minutes*

Serves *8*

450g (1lb) Brussel sprouts,
cleaned
1 Savoy cabbage, washed, with
large stalks and outer leaves
removed
3 tbs walnut oil or stir fry oil
100ml (3 fl oz) vegetable stock
2 tbs chopped walnuts

The turkey pie is quite a substantial dish but an accompaniment of shredded Brussel sprouts and Savoy cabbage completes the meal by adding texture and colour to the plate. This is also a great way to disguise the taste of Brussel sprouts – especially for children.

1 Shred the Brussel sprouts and Savoy cabbage into strips.

2 Heat a large frying pan or wok with walnut or stir fry oil.

3 Add the Brussel sprouts and Savoy cabbage and stir-fry for 3–4 minutes. Add the vegetable stock and cook for a further 3–4 minutes. Add the walnuts and continue to cook for a further 2 minutes until just soft. Serve immediately.

Saffron Lamb Tagine with Cranberries and Pistachio Nuts

Can be made in advance
Will freeze
Preparation time: *35 minutes*
Cooking time: *2½ hours*

Photograph opposite page 108

The succulent cubes of lamb that just melt in your mouth are a favourite with the whole family. The only time-consuming task is peeling the shallots, but if you plunge them into boiling water for 1 minute the skins will fall away more easily.

1   Pre-heat the oven to 170°C (325°F/gas mark 3).

2   Heat the oil and sauté the lamb in batches in a large frying pan. Remove the lamb and set aside. Fry the shallots and garlic until browned.

3   Empty the pan and fry the ginger, saffron, cinnamon, and cayenne for 1 minute. Add the flour, wine, stock and tomatoes to the spices and mix well. Bring this to the boil.

4   Transfer the lamb, onions and sauce to a large casserole dish. Cook in the oven or simmer on the hob for 2–2½ hours. The long slow cooking enhances the flavours and softens the lamb. After 1 hour add half the cranberries and all the raisins.

5   Dust individual plates with cayenne pepper. Add the tagine, scattered with pistachios, almonds and the remaining cranberries, and serve with Green Couscous and Lemon Dressing (see p.106).

Serves 8

6 tbs vegetable oil
900g (2lb) cubed shoulder of lamb
300g (10oz) shallots
4 garlic cloves, peeled and crushed
2cm (1in) fresh ginger, peeled and finely chopped
½ tsp saffron
4 tsp ground cinnamon
1 tsp cayenne pepper
3 tbs plain flour
150ml (¼ pint) red wine
900ml (1½ pints) chicken or lamb stock
1 x 400g tin (14oz) chopped tomatoes
85g (3oz) dried cranberries
85g (3oz) raisins
85g (3oz) shelled pistachio nuts
100g (4oz) whole blanched almonds, roasted

Green Couscous with Lemon Dressing

Preparation time: *5 minutes*
Cooking time: *10 minutes*

Serves 8

570ml (1 pint) vegetable or
   chicken stock
250g (9oz) couscous
3 tbs each of mint, flat-leaf
   parsley and coriander, finely
   chopped
zest and juice of 1 lemon
150ml (¼ pint) olive oil
salt and freshly ground
   black pepper

Photograph opposite page 108

1 Pour the hot stock over the couscous and cover with cling film. Leave for 10 minutes for it to absorb the stock. Add the herbs and mix well. Season with salt and freshly ground black pepper.

2 For the dressing, mix the olive oil and lemon juice together.

3 Mix all of the dressing with the couscous. The couscous is ready to serve or can be reheated later in the microwave.

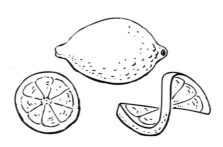

Roast Chicken with Whisky and Apricot Sauce

Can be made in advance
Will freeze
Preparation time: *30 minutes*
Cooking time: *1 hour 15 minutes*

1   Preheat the oven to 200°C (400°F/gas mark 6).

2   Place the chicken pieces, skin side down, in a roasting tin with 100ml (4fl oz) water. Scatter with the crushed garlic, fresh rosemary and lemon halves. Season with salt and freshly ground black pepper. Drizzle with the olive oil and place in the oven uncovered. Roast for 30 minutes. Turn the chicken portions over and cook for a further 45 minutes.

3   To make the mushroom base, heat the olive oil and brown sugar in a medium frying pan. Fry the whole shallots until golden brown. Add the sliced oyster mushrooms and garlic and fry over a medium heat for a further 5 minutes until the mushrooms have softened and the garlic is cooked (this can be made the day before and reheated before serving).

4   To make the sauce, marinate the apricots in the whisky overnight. Pour all the ingredients into a saucepan and reduce down by a third over a medium heat (this can be made 2 days in advance, but do keep refrigerated).

5   To serve, heat up the sauce. Heat the oyster mushroom base and divide between six plates. Sit a piece of chicken on top and pour over the apricot and whisky sauce. Serve with Mixed Wild and Red Carmargue Rice (see p.108).

Serves 6

1 large roasting chicken 2kg (4½ lb), cut into 6 portions
2 garlic cloves, peeled and crushed
6 sprigs of fresh rosemary
1 lemon, cut in half
2 tbs olive oil
salt and freshly ground black pepper

Mushroom bed
3 tbs olive oil
2 tbs brown sugar
24 shallots or baby onions, peeled
310g (11oz) oyster mushrooms, sliced
2 garlic cloves, peeled and crushed

Sauce
310g (11oz) dried apricots, cut in half
200ml (7fl oz) whisky
340g (12oz) apricot jam
juice and rind of 1 lemon

Wild and Red Carmargue Rice

Can be made in advance
Parev option
Preparation time: *5 minutes*
Cooking time: *35 minutes*

Serves 8

150g (5oz) wild rice
75g (2½oz) red Carmargue rice
40g (1½oz) margarine, melted
salt and freshly ground black
  pepper

To garnish
4 sprigs fresh rosemary

1   Bring 2 medium-sized pans of water to the boil. Add the wild rice to one and the Carmargue rice to the other.

2   Simmer both rices until tender but still with a 'bite'. The Carmargue rice will take about 25 minutes to cook and the wild rice about 35 minutes.

3   Drain both well, transfer to a serving dish and pour over the melted margarine. Mix and season well. Serve hot, garnished sprigs of with rosemary.

Saffron lamb tagine with cranberries and pistachio nuts (p. 105) served with green
couscous and lemon dressing (p. 106)

Spatchcock of poussin with caramelised apples in Somerset cider (p. 111-2) accompanied
by fondant potatoes (p. 113) and ribbons of courgette and carrot (p. 114)

Rolled spiced beef with red cabbage, curly kale (p. 116–7) and horseradish potato cakes
(p. 119)

Sole filled with salmon mousseline (p. 132–3) served with a tomato and green bean
compôte (p. 134)

Asparagus and spring onion millefeuille with grilled vegetables (p. 138–9)

Pappardelle pasta with smoked turkey, roasted fennel and orange (p. 149)

Spicy chicken masala with turmeric and saffron rice (p. 153–4), cauliflower curry and mango chutney (p. 155)

Thai fish cakes (p. 160–1) nestling on a bed of sesame vegetables (p. 162)

Honey-Glazed Chicken Breast

Can be made in advance
Suitable for Pesach (chicken only)
Preparation time: *15 minutes*
Cooking time: *40 minutes*

The whole family will love this sweet, glazed chicken recipe. Suitable accompaniments that go extremely well are sweet potato chips (or even regular chips) or mixed basmati and wild rice.

1 Preheat the oven to 200°C (400°F/gas mark 6).

2 Simmer the honey and wine together in a medium saucepan, uncovered for 10 minutes. Set aside.

3 Lightly season the chicken breasts with salt and freshly ground pepper. Dip each breast in the egg and coat with the breadcrumbs and chopped chives. Dip and coat the chicken a second time.

4 Heat the oil in a large frying pan. Fry each coated chicken breast until evenly browned on both sides.

5 Place the browned breasts in a shallow roasting tin. Pour one third of the honey glaze over the chicken. Cook for 8–10 minutes in the pre-heated oven. Remove from the oven and pour over a further third of the glaze. Return to the oven and cook for 10–15 minutes.

6 Cut the chicken breasts diagonally and fan them out on individual plates. Spoon over the remaining honey glaze and place a little bunch of watercress at the corner of the plate. Serve with Aubergine Tabbouleh (see p.110).

Serves 6

4 tbs clear honey
500ml (17fl oz) fruity red wine
6 boneless and skinless chicken breasts (supremes)
4 eggs, beaten
350g (12oz) white breadcrumbs or matzo meal
1 large bunch of chives, finely snipped
6 tbs vegetable or groundnut oil
salt and freshly ground black pepper

To garnish
1 bunch of watercress

Aubergine Tabbouleh

Can be made in advance
Preparation time: *15 minutes*
Cooking time: *15 minutes*

Serves *6*

285g (10oz) cracked wheat
4 tbs olive oil
*2 aubergines, cut into 2.5cm
    (1in) cubes*
*6 tomatoes, skinned, deseeded
    and sliced lengthways*
*juice and grated rind of
    2 lemons*
3 tbs extra virgin olive oil
*1 large bunch of parsley,
    chopped*
*salt and freshly ground
    black pepper*

This tabbouleh can be served either hot or cold. It is ideal for making in large quantities.

1 Cook the cracked wheat according to the instructions on the packet.

2 Heat the olive oil in a large saucepan and fry the aubergines until well coloured. Add the cracked wheat, tomatoes, lemon juice and rind, extra virgin olive oil and parsley to the aubergines and mix together. Season very well.

Spatchcock of Poussin with Caramelised Apples in Cider

Can be made in advance
Suitable for Pesach
Preparation time: *15 minutes*
Cooking time: *1 hour*

Photograph between pages 108 and 109

This is suitable for Rosh Hashanah or for the beginning of the Yom Kippur fast. It is easy to make for large gatherings, especially as the entire dish can be prepared in advance.

To make the Poussins

1 Preheat the oven to 200°C (400°F/gas mark 6).

2 Mix together the honey and 2 tbs vegetable oil. Brush the poussins all over evenly with honey mixture. Season well with salt and pepper.

3 Heat 2 tbs oil in a large frying pan. Fry one of the poussins for 5 minutes on each side until browned. Heat the remaining oil in the pan and fry the remaining poussin.

4 Transfer the browned poussins to a roasting tin. Pour the cider over the poussins. Bake in the oven for approximately 40 minutes (when a sharp knife is inserted and the juices run clear, the poussins are cooked).

5 Melt half the margarine in a medium-sized saucepan over a low heat. Add the sugar. Increase the heat, add the apples and toss lightly until completely golden brown.

Serves 4

4 tbs honey
6 tbs vegetable oil
2 poussins, spatchcocked
(your butcher can do this)
1.5 litre (51 fl oz) medium dry cider (use apple juice for Pesach)
30g (1oz) margarine
2 tbs demerara or soft brown sugar
3 small apples, peeled, quartered and cored (reserve the apple peelings for the sauce)
1 shallot, finely chopped
200ml (7fl oz) medium dry cider (use apple juice for Pesach)
100ml (4fl oz) white wine
salt and freshly ground black pepper

6 To make the sauce, melt the rest of the margarine in a medium-sized saucepan. Add the chopped shallot and cook for one minute until translucent but not coloured. Add the reserved apple peelings, cider and white wine. Reduce the liquid by a third. Strain the mixture into a clean pan. Check the seasoning and set aside.

7 To serve, reheat the sauce and apples. Cut each poussin in half and place on warmed plates. Spoon the sauce around each poussin and position three apple pieces on top. Accompany with Fondant Potato (see p.113) and a large spoonful of Courgette and Carrot Ribbons (see p.114).

Fondant Potatoes

Parev option
Preparation time: *10 minutes*
Cooking time: *1 hour*

Photograph between pages 108 and 109

1   Pre-heat the oven to 200°C (400°F/gas mark 6).

2   Use a 5 cm (1 in) round cutter to cut the potatoes into cylinders. If the potatoes are large, cut them in half lengthways before using the cutter. Trim both ends of the cylinder to form a barrel shape.

Serves 4

4 medium potatoes, peeled
80g (3ozs) margarine
2 tbs vegetable oil
Approx 1 litre (35fl oz) chicken
*   or vegetable stock*
4 sprigs of thyme

Remove all peel

3   Melt 25g (1oz) margarine and the vegetable oil in a frying pan and brown the potatoes evenly.

4   Transfer the potatoes to an oven-proof dish. Pour in the stock leaving the top of the potatoes just exposed. Place a knob of margarine and sprig of thyme on top of each potato. Put into the oven for 50 minutes or until soft.

Ribbon Medley of Courgettes and Carrot

Preparation time: *5 minutes*
Cooking time: *5 minutes*

Serves 4

*1 large yellow courgette – if
   unavailable use 2 green
   courgettes*
1 large green courgette
3 large carrots

Photograph between pages 108 and 109

1 Peel the carrots.

2 Top and tail the courgettes.

3 Using a peeler or a mandolin, slice into fine ribbons.
   Steam the vegetables until just cooked.

7

Sophisticated Dinner Parties

In this chapter you will find a wide
variety of sophisticated recipes, and with
careful planning and advanced
preparation you can be the relaxed
host and not spend all
evening in the kitchen.
Although they are unusual they are not
complicated. For example, the Asparagus
and Spring Onion Millefeuille with
Grilled Vegetables is stunning, tastes
fresh and delicious, blends soft and
crunchy textures together and
can be made in advance
and in stages.

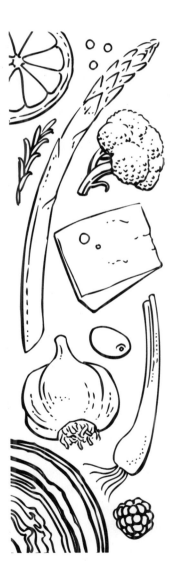

Rolled Spiced Beef with Curly Kale

Can be made in advance
Will freeze
Preparation time: *50 minutes*
Cooking time *2 hours*

Serves 4

Stuffing

2 tbs olive oil
450g (1lb) brown cap
*   mushrooms, peeled and*
*   finely chopped*
6 garlic cloves, crushed
1 slice white bread
salt and freshly ground
*   black pepper*

Spice coating

1 tsp peppercorns
6 juniper berries
4 tsp dried Chinese five spice
2 tsp coriander seeds
4 tbs plain flour
4 tbs olive oil

Rolled spice beef

4 x 140–170g (5–6oz) slices
*   of prime bola, flattened*
3 tbs vegetable oil
570ml (1 pint) fruity red wine
100g (4oz) curly kale
salt and freshly ground
*   black pepper*

Photograph between pages 108 and 109

The beef is coated in a mixture of spices, filled with a mushroom stuffing, fried and then finally cooked in the oven with red wine. The combination of spices make this a heavenly-tasting dish.

1   First make the mushroom stuffing. Heat the olive oil in a large saucepan until hot. Add the mushrooms and garlic and cook over a medium heat until the juices have been released and absorbed. Season with salt and freshly ground black pepper. Mix the bread and mushrooms together in a food processor to make a fine mixture.

2   Now prepare the spice coating. Place all the spices and the flour in a pestle and mortar and crush to a coarse powder (or use a coffee grinder).

3   Brush the flattened steaks with olive oil on one side. Coat with spices and turn it over. Spread the mushroom mixture onto the unspiced side of the steaks along the length of the meat. Carefully roll the meat lengthways and using 3–4 lengths of string, make knots to secure it. It will resemble a long sausage.

4   Heat the vegetable oil in a large frying pan. Brown
the beef parcels, one at a time so that the meat seals
fast (too many parcels at one time in the frying pan
causes the temperature to drop and stews, rather
than fries, the food).

5   Remove the parcels once they are browned. Place in
a large casserole dish. If you wish, you can
refrigerate the beef for up to 1 day before cooking.

6   Cover the meat with the red wine. Cook for 2½
hours at 170°C (325°F/gas mark 3). If you are
planning to freeze this dish, allow it to cool well
first. Defrost completely before reheating.

7   Steam the curly kale until tender.

8   Cut away the string and slice the beef parcels into
little rounds. Place the meat on the plate into a
crescent shape. Put a large spoonful of Red Cabbage
(see p.118) opposite the meat and a similar size
portion of curly kale on top. Finally stack a
Horseradish Potato Cake (see p.119) on top of the
curly kale. Spoon some red wine juices over the beef
and serve immediately.

Red Cabbage

Can be made in advance
Will freeze
Suitable for Pesach
Preparation time: *10 minutes*
Cooking time: *35 minutes*

Serves 4

450g (1lb) red cabbage, sliced
1 red apple, cored and sliced
2 red onions, finely chopped
150ml (¼ pint) red wine
300ml (½ pint) vegetable stock
110g (4oz) margarine
salt and freshly ground
  black pepper

1 Place all the ingredients together in a large saucepan.

2 Bring to the boil and lower the heat to simmer for 35 minutes or until the wine and stock have practically been absorbed. This can be made up to 2 days in advance and reheated.

Horseradish Potato Cakes

Can be made in advance
Will freeze
Parev option
Preparation time: *15 minutes*
Cooking time: *15 minutes*

Photograph between pages 108 and 109

1   Cook the potatoes in boiling water until soft. Mash the hot potatoes and allow them to dry over a low heat. Work in the polenta, margarine and flour.

2   Off the heat, add the egg, horseradish, salt and pepper. Shape into 8 cakes. Fry in a deep fat fryer for 3 minutes or until golden brown (can be reheated in the oven).

Makes 8 cakes

900g (2lb) King Edward
*   potatoes, peeled and*
*   roughly chopped*
6–8 tbs Polenta
15g (½oz) margarine
3 tbs plain flour
1 egg
1 tsp horseradish
oil for deep fat frying
salt and freshly ground
*   black pepper*

Chicken Fillet with
Garlic New Potatoes and Black Olives

Can be made in advance
Parev option
Suitable for Pesach
Preparation time: *35 minutes*
Cooking time: *1 hour*

Serves *6*

*900g (2lb) new potatoes,
    scrubbed and cut into 2.5cm
    (1 inch) chunks*
300ml (½ pint) olive oil
*340g (12oz) tomatoes, skinned
    and cut into chunks*
*200g (7oz) small onions,
    peeled, halved top to bottom*
*3 garlic cloves, peeled and finely
    chopped*
8 sprigs each thyme and sage
85g (3oz) pitted black olives
*6 tbsp groundnut or vegetable
    oil*
*6 boneless skinless chicken
    breasts*
*20g (¾oz) parsley, stems
    removed and leaves finely
    chopped*
*salt and freshly ground
    black pepper*

Parev option
red snapper
trout
salmon

1 Preheat oven to 190°C (375°F/gas mark 5). Place the potatoes in a saucepan. Cover with cold, salted water, bring to the boil and simmer for 5 minutes. Drain well.

2 Put the olive oil in a frying pan over a medium heat. Add the potatoes, tomatoes, onions, garlic, thyme and sage. Bring to the boil. Season well and simmer for 15 minutes.

3 Transfer to a casserole dish. Cook covered in the oven for 1 hour or until the potatoes are cooked through (do not stir as this will break up the vegetables). Add the olives during the last 15 minutes of cooking.

4 Heat the groundnut or vegetable oil in a large frying pan until hot. Season the chicken fillets. Fry 3 fillets at a time for 3–4 minutes on each side until they are browned. Slice each fillet into four.

5 Place the chicken slices in a covered ovenproof dish with 100ml (¼pint) of water and put in the oven 15 minutes before the potatoes will be ready.

6 To serve, stir the chopped parsley gently through the potatoes and spoon on to warmed plates. Arrange the chicken slices on top.

Sesame and Orange Lamb Chops

Preparation time: *10 minutes, plus 2 hours marinating*
Cooking time: *30 minutes*

The beauty of this dish is that it is very, very quick to make. It also tastes wonderful!

1 Mix together the sesame oil, orange juice and zest, wine, brown sugar and salt and freshly ground black pepper to make the marinade. Leave the lamb cutlets in the marinade for a minimum of 2 hours or preferably overnight in the refrigerator, turning from time to time.

2 Remove the chops from the marinade. Pour the leftover marinade into a saucepan. Bring this to the boil and reduce the liquid by a third.

3 Toast the sesame seeds by cooking in a dry saucepan until they start to colour. Turn the heat off as they will continue to cook until golden. Put to one side.

4 Heat the vegetable oil in a frying pan and fry the chops for 4–5 minutes on each side, until cooked to taste.

5 To serve, reheat the marinade. Put some Stir-fried Greens (see p.122) onto a large warmed serving plate. Arrange the chops on top with some Chunky Sweet Potato Chips (see p.123) around the edge. Spoon the reheated marinade over each chop and sprinkle with the toasted sesame seeds.

Serves 6

6 tbs sesame oil
juice and zest of 3 oranges
6 tbs red wine
3 tsp soft brown sugar
6 large lamb chops
6 tbs vegetable oil
6 tbs sesame seeds
salt and freshly ground
    black pepper

Stir-fried Greens

Preparation time: *10 minutes*
Cooking time: *10 minutes*

Serves *6*

6 tbs vegetable oil
2 tbs sesame oil
1.5kg (3lb) mixed fresh green
vegetables of your choice
(such as red chard, spinach,
broccoli, curly kale, cabbage),
finely shredded or chopped

1 Heat the oils in a wok or large saucepan.

2 Add the vegetables and stir-fry until cooked to taste.

Chunky Sweet Potato Chips

Preparation time: 10 minutes
Cooking time: 40 minutes

These chips can also be made in a deep-fat fryer in the same way as potato chips.

1 Preheat the oven to 220°C (425°F/gas mark 7).

2 Heat the oil in a large roasting tin in the oven for 10 minutes. Add the potatoes and toss until coated with oil. Bake in the oven for about 30 minutes. Shake the tin once or twice during cooking to prevent the chips from sticking. Toss with sea salt.

Serves 6

150ml (6fl oz)) sunflower oil
50ml (2fl oz) olive oil
6 large sweet potatoes, peeled
*   and cut into chunky chips*
sea salt, to taste

Crispy Duck Salad with Red Fruit

Can be made in advance
Preparation time: *30 minutes*
Cooking time: *1 hour*

Serves *6 as a starter, 4 as a main course*

4 cloves garlic, peeled and sliced
2in (5cm) fresh ginger, peeled and sliced
3 juniper berries
2.25kg (5lb) duck, cut into 4
2 litres (3 ½ pints) vegetable oil
salt and freshly ground black pepper

Dressing
90g (3oz) fresh raspberries
1 tsp light muscovado sugar
2 tbs red wine vinegar or raspberry vinegar
1 small garlic clove, peeled
½ tsp Dijon mustard
5 tbs olive oil

This dish lends itself to being made in stages. Cooking the duck, toasting the sesame seeds and making the dressing can be done up to 2 days in advance, leaving just the salad to arrange on the day of entertaining. This recipe also works well with chicken or turkey.

1 Fill a large saucepan with water and add the garlic, ginger, juniper berries and seasoning. Bring to the boil. Add the duck. Simmer with the lid on and poach for 45 minutes.

2 Remove the duck. Allow to cool slightly before removing the meat from the bone, discarding the skin. Shred the meat into large strips.

3 Heat the oil in a large pan or deep fat fryer, until hot. Fry the strips of duck until crispy (approximately 1–2 minutes). Fry in small batches so that they are crispy and keep a close eye on the frying because they can easily be overdone).

4 Put all the dressing ingredients into a food processor. Process until smooth. Check the seasoning. Sieve to remove the raspberry seeds. Refrigerate until ready to serve.

5 Arrange the salad leaves, watercress, bean sprouts and fruit on to individual large plates. Scatter over the strips of duck and chives. Drizzle with dressing and sprinkle with the roasted sesame seeds. Serve immediately.

Salad

250g (9oz) mixed salad leaves such as red oak, lambs lettuce, rocket

100g (4oz) watercress, large stalks removed

100g (4oz) beansprouts

75g (3oz) raspberries

75g (3oz) blueberries or blackcurrants

1 bunch chives, cut into 4 cm (2in) lengths

100g (4oz) sesame seeds, roasted in a dry frying pan until golden

Shoulder of Lamb Stuffed with Spinach and Raisins

Can be made in advance
Preparation time: *35 minutes*
Cooking time: *About 2 hours, depending on the weight of the lamb*

Serves 8

shoulder of lamb about 1.5–2 kg
   (3½–4½ lb), boned but
   left in one piece
300ml (½ pint) boiling water
2 glasses red wine
1 tbs brown sugar
juice of 1 orange
4 sprigs of fresh rosemary

Stuffing
1 slice of bread, toasted
1 tbs each parsley, rosemary
   and mint
300g (11oz) fresh spinach,
   trimmed, washed, chopped and
   drained or frozen leaf spinach
1 tbs olive oil
2 shallots, peeled and chopped
2 cloves garlic, peeled and
   crushed
2 tbs raisins
3 tbs pine nuts, toasted in a
   dry frying pan
zest of 1 orange
1 egg
salt and freshly ground
   black pepper

The lamb can be stuffed and prepared for roasting in the morning for an evening dinner party. You can also use the stuffing wrapped inside a chicken breast, salmon, plaice or lemon sole fillet. And for a vegetarian option, use it as part of a lasagne layer or even add to a risotto.

1 First prepare the stuffing. Make the herb breadcrumbs by combining the toast and herbs in the food processor until crumbed.

2 Cook the spinach in a dry pan, until it wilts. Squeeze all excess water out and set aside.

3 Heat the olive oil in a frying pan and sauté the shallots until softened. Add the garlic and cook for a further 2 minutes. Add the spinach, raisins, toasted pine nuts, herb breadcrumbs, orange zest, egg and seasoning to the pan and mix well. Remove from the heat.

4 Preheat the oven to 200°C (400°F/gas mark 6).

5 Lightly season the meat. Spread one side of the meat with the spinach stuffing. Fold in the 2 longer sides towards the middle and secure with several lengths of string. You should now have an elongated parcel.

6 Place the lamb parcel into a roasting tin. Pour over the boiling water, 1 glass of red wine and orange

juice. Season and add rosemary. Cook covered in the oven for 30 minutes. Baste the meat with the juices, and turn.

7   Lower the temperature to 190°C (375°F/gas mark 5) for approximately 1 hour (depending on the size of lamb and whether you like your meat rare or well done), uncovering for the last 30 minutes, after turning again.

8   Remove from the oven. Cover and leave for 10 minutes to rest.

9   Remove from the pan, cut away string and carve in to thick slices.Pour some of the excess fat from the roasting tin and discard.

10 To make the gravy, add the rest of the red wine and the brown sugar to the juices. Bring to the boil and reduce by a third until it begins to thicken a little, stirring constantly.

11 Serve slices of meat on a circle of Carrots and Red Lentils (see p.128) and pour a spoonful of gravy over them.

Carrots and Red Lentils

Can be made in advance
Parev option
Preparation time: *10 minutes*
Cooking time: *25 minutes*

Serves 8

450g (1 lb) red lentils
3 large carrots, peeled and
  finely chopped
2 tsp dried cumin
3 tsp dried coriander
3 tbs soft brown sugar
2 tbs olive oil
salt and freshly ground
  black pepper

This dish reheats well in the microwave.

1 Place the lentils and carrots into separate large saucepans.

2 Cover the lentils and carrots with water, bring each to the boil and simmer until cooked. (Approximately 15 minutes for the carrots and 10 minutes for the lentils.) The lentils should be soft but not mushy.

3 Drain each saucepan well.

4 Heat 2tbs of the olive oil in a large frying pan.

5 Add the cumin and coriander and sauté for 2 minutes to cook out the spices. (This brings out their flavour.)

6 Add the carrots to the frying pan and season with salt and freshly ground black pepper.

7 Stir in the cooked lentils and brown sugar.

8 Add the remaining olive oil and check seasoning before serving.

Salmon Pâté en Croûte

Can be made in advance
Parev option
Preparation time: *25 minutes, plus 24 hours for marinating*
Cooking time: *1 hour*

This salmon dish can be served hot or cold. It is perfect for a fancy picnic as it slices up beautifully or it could be served in small portions as a starter.

1   Marinate the trout in the wine with all the herbs, garlic and onion for 24 hours in the fridge.

2   Make a white sauce for the salmon pâté. Place the flour and 30g (1oz) butter in a saucepan. Cook for 1 minute, stirring until the butter has melted. Add the milk gradually, stirring continuously until thickened. Cover and set aside.

3   Melt the remaining butter in a saucepan. Cook the chopped mushrooms until all the butter and juices are absorbed. This will take about 15 minutes. Put the white sauce, mushrooms, eggs, puréed salmon, salt and freshly ground black pepper into a food processor. Process until smooth.

4   Carefully strain the trout, discarding the wine but keeping the other marinade ingredients. Finely chop (or use a food processor) the herbs, onion and garlic. Put the herb mixture to one side.

5   Preheat the oven to 200°C (400°F/gas mark 6).

6   Cut off a third of the pastry and save for the lid.

7   On a lightly floured surface, roll the remaining pastry

Serves: 6

2 x 150g (5oz) trout, skinned
and cut into 6 portions
100ml (3½fl oz) dry white wine
1 very large bunch of parsley,
chopped
1 large bunch each of tarragon,
oregano and thyme, chopped
3 tbs chives, snipped into short
pieces
1 clove garlic, peeled and finely
chopped
1 onion, peeled and finely chopped
300g (10oz) puff pastry
1 egg, beaten

Salmon pâté
45g (1½oz) plain flour
55g (2oz) butter or margarine
75ml (2½fl oz) milk or soya milk
for a parev option
100g (4oz) chestnut/black cap
mushrooms, roughly chopped
2 large eggs
350g (12oz) fresh salmon, puréed
in a food processor
salt and freshly ground
black pepper

129

out to line a 900g (2lb) loaf tin. Let the pastry hang over the sides as it will be trimmed away later. There is no need to grease or line the loaf tin as there is enough fat in the pastry to prevent it from sticking.

8 Fill the loaf tin with a third of the salmon mixture. Then layer with half of the herb mixture, followed by three cut trout fillets. Repeat the layering again in exactly the same order. Cover with the remaining third of the salmon mixture.

9 To make the pastry lid, roll out the reserved piece of pastry to fit the top. Brush round the edges of the pastry in the loaf tin with a little water. Place the lid over and seal all the way round. Trim the edges and use the trimmings to make pastry decorations. Glaze with egg yolk.

10 Bake for 45 minutes in the preheated oven.

11 Serve hot with a Mustard and Dill sauce (see p.131).

Mustard and Dill Sauce

Preparation time: *5 minutes*
Cooking time: *15 minutes*

This sauce is a useful accompaniment for many fish dishes. However, it will separate if it is made in advance and allowed to cool, so keep a low heat under the saucepan until ready to serve or sit in a bain marie to keep warm.

1 Bring the wine and shallots to the boil together in a medium saucepan. Simmer for 2 minutes before adding the mustard and cream. Continue to simmer for 10 minutes until the flavours have combined and the sauce has reduced by one third. Add the dill to the sauce.

2 Place in a food processor and process until combined.

3 Return the sauce to the saucepan and whisk in the butter a little at a time over a medium heat. Remove from the heat and use at once.

Serves 6

3 tbs white wine
1 shallot, peeled and finely chopped
2 tbs Dijon mustard
150ml (¼ pint) double cream
3 tbs fresh dill, roughly chopped
55g (2oz) butter, cut into cubes

131

Sole filled with Salmon Mousseline

Can be made in advance
Will freeze
Suitable for Pesach
Preparation time: *15 minutes*
Cooking time: *20 minutes*

Serves 6

340g (12oz) fresh salmon,
  boned and skinned
4 spring onions, trimmed and
  roughly chopped
2cms (1in) piece of fresh ginger,
  peeled and roughly chopped
3 tbs fresh dill
1 egg white
3 tbs whipping cream
12 fillets of lemon sole, skinned
salt and freshly ground
  black pepper

Photograph between pages 108 and 109

Although this is quick to prepare and does not require close attention during cooking, your guests will be delighted by this stunningly elegant, double fish dish. This is surely modern, stylish Jewish food at its best! For a more economical option, use plaice instead of lemon sole.

1 Place the salmon, onions, ginger and dill in the food processor and work to a paste. With the machine running, pour the egg white through the feeder tube and blend for 30 seconds. Add the cream in the same way. Season to taste. The mousseline can be refrigerated for up to 4 hours until ready to cook.

2 Spread the mousseline evenly over each sole fillet and roll up from the thick end. Secure with a cocktail stick.

3 Place in a shallow frying pan and pour in 150ml (¼ pint) water. Cover the pan and poach over a low heat for 10 minutes. Remove from the pan using a slotted spoon and drain on kitchen paper.

4 To serve, spoon a generous helping of Compôte of
Tomato and Green Bean (see p.134) on a warmed
plate. Place two sole and salmon parcels on the
plate, overlapping each other next to the compote.
Remove the cocktail sticks.

Variations

1 Make the salmon mousseline and mould into
quenelles (oval shapes) and poach for 10 minutes as
described in step 3. Serve as a starter, garnished
with salad.

2 Use approximately 12 sheets of filo pastry,
depending on the size of the sheets. Cut and shape
the filo around the parcels. Each parcel requires 3
layers of filo. Butter each layer and mould. Bake for
35 minutes at 200°C (400°F/gas mark 6) until the
pastry is golden.

Compôte of Tomatoes and Green Beans

Can be made in advance
Parev option
Preparation time: *15 minutes*
Cooking time: *20 minutes*

Serves 6

6 salad tomatoes, cut into
    quarters
12 cherry tomatoes (if possible
    6 red and 6 yellow), cut in
    half
6 plum tomatoes, cut into half
4 cloves of garlic, peeled and
    finely chopped
4 tbs extra virgin olive oil
2 tbs balsamic vinegar
110g (4oz) runner beans,
    trimmed and chopped in half
110g (4oz) fresh or frozen
    broad beans, cooked and
    skinned
110g (4oz) fine beans, trimmed
    and chopped in half
110g (4oz) mangetout, trimmed
110g (4oz) sugar snaps,
    trimmed
salt and freshly ground
    black pepper

Photograph between pages 108 and 109

Any leftovers can be used in a salad, tossed in dressing or stir-fried.

1 Preheat the oven to 200°C (400°F/gas mark 6).

2 Mix together the tomatoes, garlic, oil, balsamic vinegar, salt and freshly ground black pepper. Bake for 15 minutes in the oven until they begin to soften.

3 Steam all the beans, mangetout and sugar snaps until just soft (al dente). Drain well.

4 Remove the tomato compôte from the oven and mix with the beans. Season well.

Lime Sea Bass en Papillote

Preparation time: 30 minutes
Cooking time: 25 minutes

Cooking seabass in a parcel packed with oriental flavours perched on a bed of shredded vegetables is simplicity itself. As your guests open their individual packets they will marvel at the heady aroma of the East – and it is stylish and healthy too!

1   Preheat the oven to 200°C (400°F/gas mark 6).

2   Prepare the papillotes by cutting out 6 baking paper rectangles, large enough to wrap the fish in. Cut out 6 pieces of tin foil slightly larger than the baking paper. Place the foil rectangles on a baking tray. Put a baking paper rectangle on top of each tin foil one.

2   Mix the shredded and sliced vegetables and divide them evenly between the parchment rectangles. Sit a sea bass fillet on top of each vegetable bed. Sprinkle the zest and squeeze the juice of half a lime over each fish. Top with a kaffir lime leaf.

3   Mix the garlic, ginger, parsley, wine, soy sauce, olive oil and sesame oil together in a little dish. Spoon this equally over each fish fillet. Season with some freshly ground black pepper.

4   Seal the papillotes by folding each sides over twice and clipping them together with paper clips. Fold

Serves 6

2 leeks, washed well and shredded
2 red onions, peeled and sliced
3 heads of pak choy, finely shredded
1 red pepper, deseeded and roughly chopped
100g (4oz) baby corn, sliced in half lengthways
6 x 150g (5oz) sea bass fillets, trimmed, descaled and boned
zest and juice of 3 limes
6 kaffir lime leaves or 6 sprigs of lemon thyme
4 cloves of garlic, peeled and crushed
2 cm (1in) fresh ginger, peeled and grated
15g (½oz) flat leaf parsley
12 tbs of white wine
6 tbs of light soy sauce
3 tbs of extra virgin olive oil
3 tbs of sesame oil
freshly ground black pepper
paperclips – to fasten parcels

the centre length over twice so that it overlaps and forms a sealed parcel. Clip it together with a paper clip. Fold all the foil sides together tightly to secure all the juices inside.

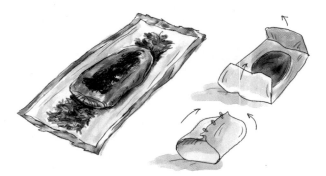

5 Bake for 25 minutes.

6 Before serving, transfer the papillotes to warmed plates, remove the paper clips and allow the guests to open their own parcels. Serve with a dish of Spring Onion Mashed Potato (see p.137).

Spring-Onion Mashed Potato

Can be made in advance
Parev option
Suitable for Pesach
Preparation time: *15* minutes
Cooking time: *25* minutes

1 Cook the potatoes in boiling salted water until tender.

2 While the potatoes are cooking, heat the olie oil in a frying pan with the olive oil and sauté the spring onions until softened.

3 Drain the potatoes, then mash. Add the fried spring onions and the butter or margarine and season to taste.

Serves 6

900g (2lb) King Edward potatoes, peeled and roughly chopped
2 tbs olive oil
2 bunches of spring onions, trimmed and roughly chopped
100g (4oz) butter or margarine
salt and freshly ground black pepper

Asparagus and Spring-Onion Millefeuille with Grilled Vegetables

Can be made in advance
Preparation time: *20 minutes*
Cooking time: *1 hour 10 minutes*

Serves 6

2 sheets ready rolled puff pastry
225g (8oz) asparagus, trimmed
2 tbsp olive oil
8 spring onions, trimmed and
*   roughly chopped*
4 large eggs
290ml (½ pint) double cream
3 tbsp fresh oregano, chopped
55g (2oz) Gruyère or strong
*   Cheddar cheese, grated*
salt and freshly ground
*   black pepper*

Photograph between pages 108 and 109

Here an asparagus and spring onion filling is sandwiched between puff pastry discs. The entire meal can be made in stages; although it takes a little time to assemble the finished dish, it is well worth the effort. A timbale is a dish named after the castle-shaped mould in which it is cooked, or any dish that is piled up high.

1   Preheat the oven to 200°C (400°F/gas mark 6).

2   Cut out 12 pastry circles using a round 10cm (4in) cutter.

3   Line a baking tray with baking paper. Place the discs on this and cover with another sheet of baking paper. Place another baking tray on top. Bake in the oven for 5 minutes.

4   Remove from the oven. Immediately gently press the top baking tray down to flatten the pastry discs. Return to the oven and cook for a further 5 minutes. Repeat the process one more time or until the pastry is golden brown and the discs are flat. These can be made up to 2 days in advance and reheated in the oven for 10 minutes at 180°C (350°F/gas mark 4).

138

5 Reduce the heat of the oven to 180°C (350°F/gas mark 4).

6 Grease 6 timbales or ramekins with a little vegetable oil or baking paper. Line the base with a circle of baking paper.

7 Steam the asparagus until cooked.

8 Heat the oil in a small frying pan and sauté the spring onions until softened.

9 In a food processor, combine the eggs, double cream, oregano, cheese and salt and freshly ground black pepper. Add the cooked asparagus and spring onions to the food processor and pulse so that the ingredients are mixed together but not puréed. Pour the vegetable mixture into the prepared ramekins or timbales and cover with a circle of greased tin foil (these can be prepared 6 hours in advance and refrigerated).

10 Sit the timbales or ramekins in a large roasting tin. Pour boiling water into the tin to come three-quarters of the way up the side of the moulds. Bake for 35 minutes or until the vegetable moulds are set.

11 Put the oil in a roasting tin and add all the vegetables. Stir to coat thoroughly and arrange in a single layer. Season with salt and pepper. Grill until the vegetables are cooked to taste. The vegetables can be cooked in advance and reheated in the oven with the pastry discs.

12 Place a hot pastry disc in the centre of a warmed plate. Invert the mould onto it. Top with a second pastry disc. Arrange the grilled vegetables around the millefeuille 'sandwich'. Drizzle on some extra virgin olive oil and sprinkle chopped basil over the vegetables.

Grilled vegetables
2 courgettes, sliced lengthways and then cut in half
2 red peppers, deseeded and cut into strips
2 yellow peppers, deseeded and cut into strips
2 red onions, peeled and cut into 12 wedges
1 large aubergine, cut into thin disc shapes
6 tbs olive oil, to glaze the vegetables
4 garlic cloves, peeled and finely chopped
salt and pepper

To garnish
4 tbs fresh basil, finely chopped
extra virgin olive oil

Cheese, Pepper and Courgette Pie

Preparation time: *40 minutes, plus 2 hours for pastry to refrigerate*
Cooking time: *1 hour 15 minutes*

Serves 8

375g (13oz) plain flour
80ml (3fl oz) olive oil
2 large eggs, lightly beaten
50ml (2fl oz) water
1 egg yolk

Filling

1kg (2lb) courgettes, sliced
  lengthways
100mls (4fl oz) olive oil
2 red peppers, deseeded and
  quartered
2 yellow peppers, deseeded and
  quartered
300g (10½oz) cream cheese
150g (5oz) herb cream cheese
5 large eggs
50g (2oz) Parmesan, grated
170g (6oz) mixed herbs (such
  as mint, basil and parsley),
  chopped
40g (1½oz) pine nuts
salt and freshly ground
  black pepper

This unusual layered pie, made with olive oil pastry, will satisfy your hungry vegetarian guests. It is a substantial, visually spectacular dish and – most important of all – a very tasty one!

1 Make the pastry by combining the flour, olive oil and whole eggs in a food processor. Gradually add the water until a firm dough ball has formed. Refrigerate, wrapped in cling film for at least 2 hours (or make a day ahead).

2 Brush the sliced courgettes with olive oil and grill them for 2 minutes on each side until golden.

3 Place the red and yellow peppers on a baking tray, brush them with olive oil and grill skin side up until the skin blisters. Immediately put the peppers in a bowl and cover them with cling film. Remove the skins when cool.

4 Using an electric mixer, beat both the cream cheeses until smooth and well combined. Continue mixing, adding the eggs one at a time. Stir in the grated Parmesan, chopped herbs and pine nuts. Season to taste.

5 Preheat the oven to 180°C (350°F/gas mark 4).

6 Cut off one third of the pastry and keep for the lid.

7 Roll out the remaining pastry to make a circle large enough to line a 24 cm (9½ in) springform or loose bottomed tin. Line the tin with the pastry, leaving the pastry to hang over the sides.

8 Spread one third of the cream cheese mixture over the pastry base and top with half the peppers and courgettes. Repeat the layering once more and finish with the remaining third of the cream cheese mixture.

9 Roll out the rest of the pastry into a circle to make a lid. Place on top and crimp the edges together, sealing well. Trim the pastry.

10 Plait the trimmings and place in a circle on the top. Glaze with egg yolk. Remove from the oven and fill the centre with pine kernels. Cook for a further 15–30 minutes until golden.

8

Midweek and Sunday Suppers

These recipes make a wonderful change
from both tired old favourites and
convenience meals. I have used more
economical ingredients that are easily
available – most may be in your
cupboard already.

They are also economical on time – both
cooking and preparation – and effort in
the kitchen. For example, Basque-style
Tuna Stew (see p.158) is all made in one
pot and a little tuna goes a very long way.

It is easy to serve and only needs
bread as an accompaniment.

Crunchy Pecan Chicken Salad

Can be made in advance
Will freeze (chicken only)
Pesach friendly
Preparation time: *40 minutes*
Cooking time: *25 minutes*

Serves 6

20g (¾oz) margarine
50g (2oz) soft brown sugar
325g (11oz) whole pecan nuts
2 slices of white bread (for
Pesach use 75g (3oz) matzo
meal)
4 skinless, boneless chicken
breasts
2 large eggs, beaten
4 tbs ground nut vegetable oil

Salad
large bunch of fresh basil
100ml (3½ fl oz) extra virgin
olive oil
1 tbs balsamic vinegar
200g (7oz) new potatoes, cut
in half
225g (8oz) asparagus, chopped
into 2cm (1in) lengths,
spears intact
1 x 200g (7oz) bag of mixed
salad leaves
3 small avocados
salt and freshly ground
black pepper

This delicious, interesting salad main course, which can be prepared in stages, is perfect for a hot summer's day.

1 To caramelise the pecan puts, melt the margarine and sugar together in a small saucepan. Add 100g (4oz) of the pecans and cook until the sugar starts to caramelise into a rich brown colour. Turn out onto baking parchment and allow to cool.

2 Pre-heat oven to 200°C (400°F/gas mark 6).

3 Make the coating by processing the bread and the rest of the pecans in the food processor (or chop by hand).

4 Dip the chicken breasts into the beaten egg followed by the breadcrumb mixture. Repeat process to give a really crunchy coating. These can be refrigerated for up to 4 hours until ready to fry.

5 Heat the groundnut or vegetable oil in a frying pan. Fry the coated chicken for 2–3 minutes on each side so it is nicely browned but not burnt. (If the oil starts to burn, discard it, clean the pan and start frying again with fresh oil.)

6 Place the chicken breasts on a baking tray lined with baking parchment. Complete the cooking in the oven for 15 minutes.

7 Finely chop the basil in a food processor or blender. Gradually add the olive oil, balsamic vinegar, salt and pepper.

8 Boil the potatoes until cooked. Drain the potatoes and return them to the pan. While they are still hot, cover with the dressing, mix and set aside. This can be completed up to 4 hours in advance.

9 Steam the asparagus until just cooked. Mix with the dressed potatoes and salad leaves.

10 Peel the avocados, remove the stones and slice. Place the dressed salad on to individual dinner plate. Slice the warm chicken breasts. Arrange the chicken and avocado slices alternately in a semi-circle. Drizzle any excess dressing over the salad, then sprinkle the caramelised pecans on top. Serve immediately.

Crispy Turkey Loaf

Can be made in advance
Can freeze
Suitable for Pesach
Preparation time: *20 minutes*
Cooking time: *1 hour*

Serves 6

1–2 tbs olive oil
1 red onion, peeled and
  roughly chopped
2 courgettes, sliced into circles
outer leaves of a savoy cabbage,
  washed thoroughly
450g (1 lb) minced turkey
2 slices white bread, made into
  breadcrumbs (for Pesach use
  75g (3oz) mata meal)
1 egg
2 tbs redcurrant jelly
1 bunch fresh mint
2 tbs sun-dried tomato purée
3 salad tomatoes, sliced
salt and freshly ground
  black pepper

This is an unusual and economical way of using mince. The crispy coating has a wonderful crunchy texture.

1 Preheat the oven to 180°C (375°F/gas mark 5).

2 Heat the olive oil in a frying pan and sauté the onion until it is softened but not coloured. Remove the onion and set aside.

3 Using the same pan, adding more olive oil if needed, lightly fry the sliced courgettes for 30 seconds on each side so that they are still firm but slightly cooked.

4 Using a sharp knife, cut the thick stalks out of the outer green cabbage leaves. Line a 900g (2lb) loaf tin with the prepared cabbage leaves, leaving enough overhang to be able to cover the loaf tin.

5 Put the minced turkey, breadcrumbs, egg, redcurrant jelly, fresh mint, tomato purée and sautéed onion in the food processor. Season generously with salt and freshly ground black pepper. Process to a paste.

6 Spoon half the turkey mixture into the prepared loaf tin. Place all the sliced courgettes in a layer on top of the mince, followed by a layer of all the sliced tomatoes. Spoon the rest of the turkey mixture on

the top. Fold over the overhanging cabbage leaves and cover with greased tin foil. Bake for 50 minutes or until firm to touch.

7 Remove from the oven and carefully drain away the excess liquid. Discard the tin foil and invert onto an ovenproof platter. Return to the oven for 10 minutes to crisp up the outer cabbage layer.

8 Serve with jacket potatoes and Tomato Salsa (see p.148).

Tomato Salsa

Can be made in advance
Parev option
Suitable for Pesach
Preparation time: *5 minutes*

Serves 6

2 red peppers, deseeded
4 salad tomatoes
1 bunch coriander, trimmed
½ red onion, peeled
2 tbs extra virgin olive oil
*1 tbs freshly squeezed lemon
    juice*
*2 pieces of sun-dried tomato
    in olive oil*
*salt and freshly ground
    black pepper*

You can make this versatile relish in advance and keep it for up to two days in the fridge. It is the perfect accompaniment for Indian, Mexican, Spanish and American dishes and it is great with crisps or crudités.

1 Place all the ingredients into a food processor. Pulse carefully until the ingredients are very finely chopped and combined.

2 Refrigerate until chilled.

Individual raspberry cheesecakes (p. 168-9)

Soft fruit tart (p. 175-6)

Pappardelle Pasta with Smoked Turkey, Roasted Fennel and Orange

Can be made in advance
Preparation time: *25 minutes*
Cooking time: *20 minutes*

Photograph between pages 108 and 109

This is a really quick, creative meal. Smoked turkey is now available from your local butcher but smoked chicken or cooked chicken can be substituted. Pappardelle are broad noodles traditionally served with game – fresh or dried can be used. If pappardelle is not available, use tagliatelli. For a vegetarian option, omit the turkey and add 225g (8oz) of cooked asparagus and 110g (4oz) feta cheese.

1 Preheat the oven to 200°C (400°F/gas mark 6).

2 Remove the outer leaves of the fennel and chop roughly. Drizzle with the olive oil and roast in the oven for 20 minutes.

4 Zest 4 of the oranges and then peel, making sure that most of the pith is removed. Using a sharp knife, cut between the membranes and remove the orange segments.

5 Cook the pasta according to the packet instructions. Drain. Return it to the cooking pan. Toss it in the juice of 1 orange and the extra virgin olive oil. Season well. Add the cubed turkey, roasted fennel, segmented oranges, chopped chives and the trimmed watercress. Mix well.

6 Serve immediately in a large bowl. Sprinkle over some soya Parmesan.

Serves 6

2 fennel bulbs
3 tbs olive oil
5 oranges
500–600g (1lb) pappardelle pasta
3 tbs extra virgin olive oil
6 thick slices of smoked turkey, cut into bite-size cubes
1 bunch of chives, chopped into 1cm (½ in) lengths
1 large bunch of watercress, trimmed
soya Parmesan, optional
salt and freshly ground black pepper

Pan-Fried Calf Liver

Can be made in advance
Suitable for Pesach *(liver and relish only)*
Preparation time: *10 minutes*
Cooking time: *15 minutes*

Serves 4

*4 tbs plain flour or fine
    matza meal*
*4 slices of koshered calfs' liver
    (or ox liver, if preferred)*
55g (2oz) margarine
4 tbs olive oil
*salt and freshly ground
    black pepper*

To garnish
flat-leaf parsley

Liver is an acquired taste but for those that like it, it is a favourite. Be careful not to over cook otherwise it will be tough and chewy!!

1   Season the flour with salt and freshly ground black pepper. Coat the liver with the seasoned flour.

2   Melt the margarine together with the oil until the fat starts to foam. Fry the liver for about 3 minutes on each side. Remove and serve immediately on a bed of Mustard Mashed Potato (see p.151), with a generous side-helping of Beetroot and Red Onion Relish (see p.152). Top with the flat-leaf parsley.

Mustard Mashed Potato

Can be made in advance
Parev option
Preparation time: *10 minutes*
Cooking time: *20 minutes*

This can be made up to one day in advance, refrigerated and reheated in the microwave for 4 minutes.

1 Peel and chop the potatoes. Cook the potatoes in boiling, salted water until tender. Drain and return to the hot empty pan.

2 Mash until the potatoes are soft, creamy and free from lumps. Add the margarine, mustard and seasoning, and mix well.

Serves 4

900g (2lb) potatoes
75g (3oz) margarine, cut into
   cubes
2 tbs whole grain mustard
salt and freshly ground
   black pepper

Beetroot and Red Onion Relish

Can be made in advance
Parev option
Suitable for Pesach
Preparation time: *10 minutes*
Cooking time: *30 minutes*

Serves 4

2 tbs vegetable oil
225g (8oz) red onions, peeled
and thinly sliced
150ml (¼ pint) red table wine
juice and zest of 2 oranges
1 cm (½ inch) piece of fresh
root ginger, peeled and
grated
1½ tsp brown sugar
100ml (4fl oz) kiddush wine
75g (3oz) cooked beetroot,
chopped into matchstick
pieces
salt and freshly ground
black pepper

This relish makes an excellent accompaniment to most poultry dishes and cold meats. It can be made up to 2 days in advance and stored in an airtight container in the refrigerator.

1 Heat the oil in a frying pan and fry the onions, covered, over a low heat until soft and caramelised, stirring occasionally. This will take about 20 minutes.

2 Add the red table wine and orange juice to the onions. Bring to the boil. Simmer until the liquid is almost reduced to nothing. This will take about 5 minutes. Add the ginger, orange zest, sugar and kiddush wine. Bring to the boil and simmer again until syrupy. This will take about 5 minutes. Add the chopped beetroot.

3 Season to taste and mix well.

Spicy Chicken Masala with Turmeric and Saffron Rice

Can be made in advance
Preparation time: *25 minutes, plus marinating the chicken either overnight or minimum time of 2 hours*
Cooking time: *35 minutes*

Photograph between pages 108 and 109

The spice in this dish can adjusted to your own taste by altering the amount of chilli and curry powder. Corn bread (see p.153–154) goes particularly well with this meal, or offer a selection of spicy crisps.

1 To marinate the chicken, combine all the marinade ingredients and pour over the chicken. Leave for a minimum of two hours or overnight in the refrigerator.

2 Pre-heat oven to 180°C (350°F/gas mark 4).

3 Put the rice and salt in a large saucepan with the water and bring to the boil.

4 Add the turmeric and saffron. Simmer for 10–15 minutes, until all the water has been absorbed and the rice is soft. Check the seasoning.

5 Grease 6 timbales (or ramekins or individual pudding basins) with a little vegetable oil. Fill with the cooked rice. Make 6 foil circles to act as lids, grease with vegetable oil and seal over each timbale.

6 Sit each covered timbale in a large roasting tin. Fill the roasting tin half way up with boiling water to make a bain marie. Place the bain marie in the oven and cook for 10–15 minutes. To make the rice in

Serves 6

6 boneless, skinless chicken breasts

Marinade
zest and juice of 1 lemon
zest and juice of 1 lime
2 cloves garlic, peeled and finely sliced
1 tsp salt
1 tsp curry powder (medium strength)
1 tbs chilli oil or olive oil
1 small red chilli, halved, de-seeded and chopped
2 tbs clear honey
2 tbs fresh coriander, chopped

Rice
330g (10oz) basmati rice
1 tsp salt
570ml (1 pint) water
½ tsp turmeric
4 saffron threads

To garnish
coriander leaves
slices of lime, twisted

advance, complete until the end of stage 6 and refrigerate for up to 4 hours.

6 Remove the chicken from the marinade and grill for 15–20 minutes until golden, basting from time to time with the excess marinade.

7 Slice the chicken diagonally so that you can fan it out on to individual plates. plate and place a timbale rice next to it. Serve with some Cauliflower Curry and Mango Chutney (see p.155). To finish, decorate with the coriander leaves and a twist of lime.

Cauliflower Curry and Mango Chutney

Can be made in advance
Preparation time: *25 minutes*
Cooking time: *15 minutes*

Photograph between pages 108 and 109

The sweetness of the chutney perfectly complements the spicy vegetable curry. Make a larger quantity of the curry for a tasty, light supper.

1 To make the chutney, combine all the ingredients, except the fresh coriander, stir, and refrigerate until ready to serve. This can be made up to 24 hours in advance (add the coriander just before seving).

2 Crush all the ingredients for the curry paste in a pestle and mortar or coffee grinder.

3 Cook the potatoes and cauliflower separately in boiling salted water until tender. Drain well.

4 Heat the vegetable oil and add the curry paste. Cook for 1–2 minutes until the flavours are well absorbed together. Add the chopped tomatoes, cauliflower and potatoes. Mix together and reheat when ready to serve.

Mango chutney
1 tbs extra virgin olive oil
juice of 1 lime
1 ripe mango, peeled and finely cubed
½ each yellow and orange pepper, diced
1 green chilli, deseeded and chopped
1 bunch of coriander, finely chopped
2 tbs mango chutney
2 garlic cloves, peeled and finely chopped
2cm (1in) ginger, peeled and grated

Curry paste
3 garlic cloves, peeled and roughly chopped
10 cardamon seeds
8 black peppercorns
2 tsp coriander seeds
2 tsp cinnamon
1 tsp chilli powder

Cauliflower curry
350g (12oz) potatoes, peeled and chopped into cubes
250g (9oz) cauliflower, cut into florets
7 medium-sized tomatoes, roughly chopped
3 tbs vegetable oil

Smoked Fish with Pasta and Roasted Vegetables

Can be made in advance
Parev option
Preparation time: *20 minutes*
Cooking time: *30 minutes*

Serves *4*

1 each red and yellow pepper, deseeded and roughly chopped
1 red onion, peeled and chopped into large chunks
6 tbs olive oil
4 cloves of garlic, peeled and crushed
300g (11oz) dried pasta shapes
150g (5oz) sugar snaps, trimmed
100g (4oz) asparagus, trimmed and cut into 5 cm (2 in) lengths
75g (3oz) broad beans, fresh or frozen
4 x 150g (5oz) fillets of smoked fish, skin removed and cut into bite-size pieces
salt and freshly ground black pepper

There are many different options from which to choose your smoked fish for this recipe. I particularly like oak smoked salmon as its colour and subtle flavour enhances the pasta effectively. Smoked trout, smoked mackerel, smoked halibut or smoked cod could also be used – see what is available at your local fishmongers. Serve this hot, cold or warm.

1 Preheat the oven to 200°C (400°F/gas mark 6).

2 Place the peppers and onion on a roasting tin and drizzle with the olive oil. Sprinkle with the crushed garlic and salt and freshly ground black pepper. Roast for 15–20 minutes.

3 Bring a large pan of salted water to the boil. Add the dried pasta and cook according to the packet instructions (approximately 10–14 minutes) until the pasta is al dente. Drain and transfer to a large serving dish.

4 Steam, blanch or microwave the sugar snaps and asparagus until just cooked. Drain and plunge into cold water and drain again.

5 Cook the broad beans in boiling water for 2 minutes. Drain and remove the skins. (Skinning cooked, fresh broad beans may seem a laborious task but once you have seen the difference in colour and shape from frozen or tinned, you will agree it was well worth the effort.)

6 Mix the roasted vegetables and all their juices, the sugar snaps, asparagus and broad beans into the pasta. Season to taste. Mix in the fish carefully to prevent it from breaking up. Serve immediately.

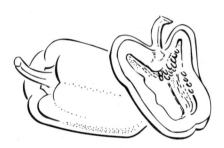

Basque-style Tuna Stew

Can be made in advance
Parev option
Will freeze
Preparation time: *30 minutes*
Cooking time: *40 minutes*

Serves 6

6 tbs olive oil

*2 onions, peeled and roughly
   chopped*

*1 each red and yellow pepper,
   deseeded and roughly chopped*

*1 large aubergine, cut into 2cm
   (1in) cubes*

1 tbs paprika

*1x395g (14oz) tin chopped
   tomatoes*

*2 tbs sun-dried tomatoes,
   chopped*

4 cloves garlic, peeled and sliced

150ml (¼ pint) red wine

*4 Desirée potatoes, peeled and
   cut into 2cm (1in) cubes*

3 fresh bay leaves

*1 unwaxed lemon, cut into
   quarters*

*2 sprigs lemon thyme
   (if available)*

*900ml (1½ pints) vegetable or
   fish stock*

This is a quick and delicious stew made in one pot. Serve with some crusty bread or a filling meal.

1   Heat the olive oil in a large, heavy-based saucepan. Sauté the onions and peppers for 5 minutes. Add the aubergine and continue cooking until all the vegetables are softened. Add the paprika. Stir over the heat for 30 seconds.

2   Add the tomatoes with their juice, chopped sun-dried tomatoes, sliced garlic, red wine, potatoes, bay leaves, the lemon, the thyme, all the stock and salt and freshly ground black pepper to taste. Simmer, uncovered, over a medium heat for about 20 minutes until the potatoes are tender. (This can be made as far as this stage a day in advance, cooled and refrigerated.)

3   Stir in the tuna and anchovies. Cook for a further 2 minutes. Remove from the heat. Cover the stew with a lid. Stand for 5 minutes before checking the seasoning and serving.

4 Ladle into deep bowls and garnish with the flat leaf parsley. Serve with chunks of crusty bread.

Variation

Omit the tuna and anchovies and replace with 4 boneless, skinless chicken breasts cut into 2 cm (1 in) cubes. Add with the tomatoes in step 2 and cook for 20 minutes and continue with the rest of the recipe.

salt and freshly ground
  black pepper
750g (1½lb) fresh tuna, cut into
  2cm (1in) cubes
1 small jar garlic and herb
  anchovies or plain anchovies,
  drained

To garnish
1 bunch of flat-leaf parsley

Thai Fish Cakes

Can be made in advance
Will freeze (fishcakes only)
Parev option
Preparation time: *30 minutes, plus 1 hour chilling*
Cooking time: *30 minutes*

Serves 6

450g (1lb) cod or other white
*   fish fillet, skinned, boned and*
*   cubed*
milk to cover the fish (use soya
*   milk for a parev option)*
2 lime leaves (if available)
50g (2oz) unsalted butter (use
*   margarine for a parev option)*
50g (2oz) plain flour
4 spring onions, trimmed
2 red chillies, deseeded and
*   chopped*
2 garlic cloves, peeled
2cm (1in) fresh ginger, peeled
*   and finely chopped*
15g (½oz) fresh coriander
110g (4oz) white bread
1 egg white, lightly whisked
4 tbsp shredded coconut
170g (5oz) white bread
15g (½oz) fresh coriander
110g (4oz) plain flour
vegetable oil
2 eggs, lightly beaten
salt and freshly ground
*   black pepper*

Photograph opposite page 109

These fish cakes are very popular and you will make them time and time again. Try serving one as a starter. They are even a favourite with children!!

1   Put the cubed fish into a shallow pan and cover with milk. Add the lime leaves. Bring to the boil and simmer for 3–4 minutes. Strain the fish, reserving 125ml (4fl oz) of the milk. Remove the lime leaves.

2   Next, make the white sauce. Melt the butter in a small pan. Add the flour. Cook, stirring for 1 minute. Beat in the milk slowly until smooth. Set aside.

3   Put the fish into a food processor. Add the spring onions, chillies, garlic, ginger, coriander, bread, whisked egg white, plenty of salt and freshly ground black pepper, and the white sauce. Process until mixed but not puréed. Stir in the shredded coconut.

4   With floured hands shape the mixture into round cakes, using approximately 2 tbs for each. Put on to a floured plate and chill in the fridge for 1 hour.

5 Process the bread and coriander in a food processor to make breadcrumbs.

6 Heat the oil in a deep-fat fryer.

7 Coat each fishcake in flour, beaten egg and finally the coriander breadcrumbs.

8 Fry the fish cakes for 3–4 minutes until golden. Drain on absorbent paper.

9 Deep fry the coriander leaves for 10 seconds and remove. Drain on absorbent paper.

10 Sit a fish cake on a bed of Sesame Vegetables (see p.162), and serve with a few deep-fried coriander leaves and a wedge of lime.

To garnish
*1 small bunch of coriander
  leaves*
1 lime, cut into wedges

Sesame Vegetables

Can be made in advance
Parev option
Preparation time: *10 minutes*
Cooking time: *7 minutes*

Serves 6

2 tbs sesame oil
1 fennel bulb, finely chopped
½ red onion, peeled and
  finely chopped
½ red pepper, deseeded and
  finely chopped
225g (8oz) shitake or oyster
  mushrooms, sliced
200g (7oz) leaf spinach,
  washed and shredded
2 tbs soy sauce
1 tbs brown sugar
1 tbs sesame seeds

Photograph opposite page 109

1 Heat the sesame oil in a large saucepan or wok.

2 Stir fry the fennel, red onion and red pepper for 2–3 minutes. Add the mushrooms, spinach, soy sauce and brown sugar. Continue cooking for a further 3 minutes.

3 Sprinkle with sesame seeds before serving.

Tomato and Feta Cheese Bread Salad

Preparation time: 10 minutes, plus 15 minutes standing time

This is really quick and a delicious family favourite and can be served as an accompaniment with fish or as a main course with a green salad.

1   Put the olive oil, vinegar, garlic paste, salt and plenty of fresh ground black pepper into your serving bowl. Add the bread and mix. Add all the remaining ingredients.

2   Toss to combine well, taking care not to break up the feta cheese. Let the salad stand at room temperature for a minimum of 15 minutes to allow the bread to soak up some of the dressing.

3   Serve with green salad leaves, including baby spinach leaves, rocket or watercress.

Serves 6

200ml (7fl oz) extra virgin
   olive oil
3 tbs red wine vinegar
4 cloves garlic, peeled and
   crushed to a paste
340g (12oz) crusty bread or
   left-over challah, cubed
310g (11oz) red cherry
   tomatoes, halved (or salad
   tomatoes cut into wedges)
310g (11oz) yellow cherry
   tomatoes (if available or use
   more red), halved
150g (5oz) black olives, halved
30g (1oz) fresh basil, finely
   chopped
200g (7oz) feta cheese, cubed
salt and freshly ground black
   pepper

Aubergine Schnitzel with Coriander Pesto Dressing

Can be made in advance
Preparation time: *45 minutes*
Cooking time: *30 minutes*

Serves 6

450g (1lb) white bread
6 tbs parsley
3–4 medium sized aubergines,
  cut lengthways into ½ cm
  (¼ in) slices
6 eggs, lightly beaten
100ml (4fl oz) vegetable oil
500g (1lb) plum tomatoes,
  sliced
4 tbs extra virgin olive oil
6 cloves of garlic, peeled and
  finely chopped
6 tbs fresh chopped coriander
100g (4oz) pine nuts, toasted in
  a dry frying pan
30g (1oz) Parmesan, grated
150ml (¼ pint) olive oil
110g (4oz) Gruyère cheese,
  grated
extra virgin olive oil
salt and freshly ground
  black pepper

Aubergines are a very versatile vegetable and this unusual way of cooking them captures all their flavour and texture. This recipe is recommended to satisfy your vegetarian guests.

1 Preheat the oven to 200°C (400°F/gas mark 6).

2 Put the bread and parsley into the food processor and process to produce parsley breadcrumbs.

3 Dip the sliced aubergine first in the beaten egg, and then in the parsley breadcrumbs. Repeat to produce a really good coating.

4 Heat a large frying/griddle pan with about 4 tbs of the vegetable oil (add more oil as required). Drain on absorbent paper to cool.

5 Place the plum tomatoes on a baking sheet. Sprinkle with the extra virgin olive oil, chopped garlic, salt and freshly ground black pepper. Bake the seasoned tomatoes for 15 minutes in the pre-heated oven.

6 To make the pesto place the coriander, toasted pine nuts, Parmesan and salt and freshly ground black pepper in the food processor and mix well. While the machine is running, gradually pour in the olive oil. This can be made up to 2 days in advance and refrigerated.

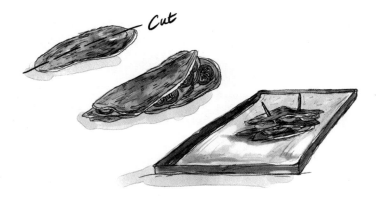

7 Pre-heat the oven to 200°C (400°F/gas mark 6).

8 Cut each aubergine slice in half diagonally and place on a baking tray lined with baking parchment. Place 4–5 slices of tomato on each aubergine half slice. Sprinkle with some grated Gruyère cheese, salt and freshly ground black pepper, and a drizzle of extra virgin olive oil. Cover with the other half slice. Repeat the same filling, followed by one more aubergine slice so that you have a three-aubergine-layered stack. Skewer each schnitzel with two cocktail sticks to secure. Bake the aubergine schitzels for 15 minutes.

9 Place each aubergine schnitzel on to a warmed plate. Drizzle with the coriander pesto dressing and serve immediately with a green salad.

9

Desserts

In putting together this collection of desserts I have tried to make as many as possible Parev to allow you the flexibility of serving them whenever you choose. Many are great for Pesach — I have not compromised on taste when using dairy substitute, kosher margarines or kosher for Pesach ingredients. On the contrary, lime mousse tastes better with soya cream than fresh cream and is healthier. With current prevalence of the nut and dairy allergies you will still be able to find something here to satisfy everyone's sweet tooth.

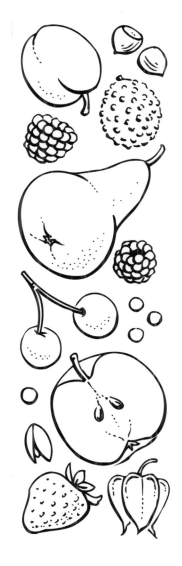

Individual Raspberry Cheesecakes

Can be made in advance
Suitable for Pesach
Preparation time: *40 minutes, plus 1 hour cooling time; 2 hours or overnight chilling time*
Cooking time: *25 minutes*

Serves 8

750g (1½lb) curd cheese
5 tbs caster sugar
3 eggs, separated
1 tbs plain flour
grated zest of 2 lemons, plus the
  juice of 1 lemon
seeds from a vanilla pod or
  1 tsp vanilla essence
125g (4½oz) fresh raspberries

To garnish
1 packet fresh mint
icing sugar
100g (4oz) toasted flaked
  almonds
125g (4½oz) fresh raspberries

Photograph opposite page 148

These little cheesecakes are made in advance and are easy to serve. Blueberries or raisins soaked in brandy can be substituted for fresh raspberries for a change. If you prefer, make one large cake using a deep 22–25cm (8–9in) loose-bottom, springform tin. To make these cheesecakes for Pesach, use potato flour instead of plain flour, and cream cheese instead of curd cheese.

1 Heat the oven to 190°C (375°F/gas mark 5).

2 Grease the base and sides of 8 ramekins with butter and line the base of each one with a circle of baking paper. Dust inside each one with caster sugar – shake out any surplus put 7 raspberries into the base of each ramekin.

3 Beat together the curd cheese, sugar, egg yolks, flour, lemon zest, lemon juice and vanilla seeds or essence.

4 Whisk the egg whites until stiff peaks are formed. Fold one spoonful of egg white into the curd mixture to lighten it using a large metal spoon. Fold in the remainder gently but thoroughly.

5 Fill each ramekin with the cheese mixture.

6 Put the ramekins into a roasting tin filled with boiling water (bain marie) in the oven for 25 minutes or until set.

7 Turn off the oven and leave the cakes to cool in the oven for 1 hour. This stops the surface from cracking and works for any baked cheesecake. Chill in the fridge for at least 2 hours or preferably overnight.

8 Invert the cheesecakes on to a dark-coloured plate so that it sits upwards, peel off the baking paper and dust with icing sugar. Decorate the tops with toasted flaked almonds and arrange a layer of raspberries around the base of each one.

Fruits of the Forest Brûlée

Can be made in advance
Will freeze
Suitable for Pesach
Preparation time: *45 minutes, plus 5 hours overnight chilling time*
Cooking time: *10 minutes*

Serves 6

450g (1lb) packet frozen
summer fruits or fresh red soft
fruits – for Pesach option
600 ml (1 pint) double cream
1 cinnamon stick or 1 tsp
ground cinnamon
3 egg yolks
50g (2oz) caster sugar
30g (1oz) cornflour or potato
flour
approx 8 tbs each of icing sugar
and demerara sugar

This is a great favourite – despite the calories – and a particularly good dessert for Pesach. It can be made individually or in one large deep serving dish.

1 Defrost the summer fruits thoroughly, drain well and discard the juices.

2 Bring the double cream to the boil with the cinnamon in a large saucepan. Set the mixture aside for 10 minutes, then remove the cinnamon stick if used and discard.

3 Whisk together the egg yolks, caster sugar and the cornflour until pale and thick. This helps to stabilise the mixture and prevent it from curdling.

4 Pour the cinnamon-infused cream into the egg mixture and whisk to combine. Return the mixture to the saucepan. Stir over a moderate heat for 5–10 minutes – but do not boil – until the mixture has thickened in the pan and will coat the back of a wooden spoon.

5 Divide the summer fruits mixture equally between 6 ramekins.

6 Sieve the thickened cream into a large jug. Carefully pour into each ramekin, filling them evenly. Leave the mixture to chill in the fridge for at least 4 hours or overnight. The desserts can be frozen at this stage.

7 Completely cover each ramekin with icing sugar. Place under a fierce grill for 2–3 minutes, or until the sugar has melted and is bubbling on the top. Remove immediately.

8 Completely cover with demerara sugar. Grill again until the topping is shiny and caramelised.

9 Chill in the refrigerator for at least 1 hour before serving.

Plum and Apricot Tatin

Can be made in advance
Parev option
Preparation time: *35 minutes*
Cooking time: *25 minutes*

Serves 8

150g (5ozs) caster sugar
1 tbs water
10 medium plums, halved and
stoned
10 apricots, halved and stoned
2 tsp ground mixed spice
450g (1lb) puff pastry
1 beaten egg yolk

This is an ideal family dessert to follow a chicken meal.

1 Preheat the oven to 220°C (425°F/gas mark 7).

2 Put the sugar and water in to a 26cm (10in frying pan. If your pan is not ovenproof, transfer the fruit to an ovenproof dish after step 3.

3 Arrange the plums and apricots skin-side down to cover the base of the pan. Simmer over a medium heat for 15–20 minutes until the plums and apricots start to soften and the sugar begins to caramelise. Remove from the heat and pour away any excess juice. Sprinkle the fruit evenly with the ground mixed spice.

4 Roll the puff pastry to a circle slightly larger than the frying pan. Place the puff pastry over the frying pan and tuck in round the edge. Glaze the pastry with the beaten egg yolk.

5 Bake for 20 minutes or until the pastry is golden. Remove and allow to cool for 5 minutes. Drain any excess juice off carefully if necessary.

6 To turn out, cover the pan with a large curved serving plate and invert.

7 Serve with double cream or vanilla ice cream, or with parev ice cream if you are having a meat meal.

Double-chocolate baked Alaska (p. 181)

Parev hazelnut ice cream (p. 191-2) and crunchy nut biscotti with red fruit compôte (p. 184–5)

Bread and Butter Pudding

Can be made in advance
Will freeze
Preparation time: *25 minutes*
Cooking time: *35 minutes*

Some bread and butter puddings are on the heavy side but this recipe is very light and fluffy. In fact, it's so utterly delicious that second helpings are sure to be requested.

1 Preheat the oven to 180°C (350°F/gas mark 4).

2 Soak the sultanas in the Cointreau.

3 Put the milk, cream and split vanilla pod in a large saucepan. Bring to the boil. Remove from heat and allow to infuse for 10 minutes.

4 Grease a medium oval dish.

5 Cut the bread rolls into thin slices and butter. Line the base of the dish with the bread, buttered side down. Sprinkle the bread evenly with the soaked sultanas.

6 Whisk the eggs and sugar together until pale and thick.

7 Remove the split vanilla pod from the milk. Add the milk mixture to the egg mixture and whisk briefly until just combined. Pour this over the bread and leave for 5 minutes to let the custard soak in.

8 Place the dish in a roasting tin and fill it with boiling

Serves 6

50g (2oz) sultanas
2 tbs Cointreau
250ml (9fl oz) full-fat milk
250ml (9fl oz) double cream
1 vanilla pod, split lengthways
6 soft white bread rolls
40g (1½oz) butter, softened
3 large eggs
150g (5oz) caster sugar
50g (2oz) apricot jam
a little icing sugar

water to come half way up the oval dish (bain marie). Bake for 35 minutes.

9   Melt and sieve the apricot jam to make a glaze. Brush the top of the pudding with the glaze. Dust with icing sugar. Put the dish under a hot grill until the top is golden brown. You can make this dish up to this stage, 24 hours in advance. Store in the refrigerator and reheat in the oven.

10 Dust with icing sugar and serve.

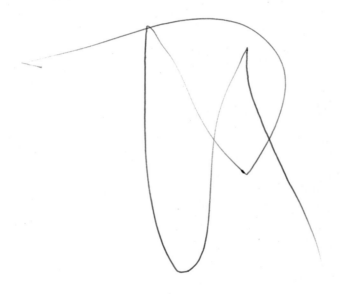

Soft Fruit Tart

Can be made in advance
Will freeze (pastry only)
Parev option
Preparation time: *40 minutes, plus 30 minutes for refrigerating the pastry*
Cooking time: *25 minutes*

Photograph opposite page 149

This eye-catching, multi-coloured dessert makes a glamorous centrepiece for any dessert buffet table. The recipe also adapts well if you choose to make individual tarts. The parev version, with crème patissiere instead of fromage frais, is just as impressive. Do vary the fruits to take advantage of seasonal availability.

1 Preheat the oven to 200°C (400°F/gas mark 6).

2 To make the pastry, put the butter, flour, sugar, lemon zest and juice, and whole egg in a food processor. Process until a ball of pastry has formed. Flatten and wrap in clingfilm. Refrigerate for 30 minutes.

3 Roll the pastry out on a lightly floured surface to fit a 25cm (10in) loose-bottomed tart tin. Line the tin with the pastry. Bake blind by covering the raw pastry with tin foil (including the edges) and filling with baking beans or dried pulses. Cook for 20 minutes.

Serves 8–10

140g (5oz) butter (use margarine for the parev option), softened
260g (9oz) plain flour
40g (1½oz) caster sugar
zest of 1 lemon, plus 1 tbs lemon juice
1 egg
1 egg yolk, beaten
1 jar apricot jam
150 ml (¼ pint) no fat fromage frais mixed with 3 tbs icing sugar
approx 900g (2lb) selection of soft seasonal fruits (such as apricots, plums, physalis, mango, strawberries, dates, blueberries, raspberries, peaches, blackberries, nectarines)

Parev option

3 egg yolks

70g (2 ½oz) caster sugar

250 ml (9fl oz) soya cream

1 split vanilla pod or 1 tsp vanilla essence

1 tbs custard powder

20g (¾oz) plain flour

4 Remove the foil and baking beans and glaze the pastry with the beaten egg yolk. Return the pastry to the oven for 5 minutes or until golden brown.

5 Melt and sieve the apricot jam to make a glaze. Glaze the pastry with some of the warmed glaze.

6 Prepare the fruit as if for a fruit salad.

7 Mix the fromage frais with the icing sugar then spread on to the cooled pastry case. Spoon on the prepared soft fruits in a higgledy-piggledy fashion. Brush the fruit with warmed apricot glaze.

Parev alternative

1 Beat the eggs and sugar together until pale and thick.

2 Bring the soya cream to the boil with the split vanilla pod or essence.

3 Take 1 tbs of the cream and mix with the custard powder and flour to form a paste. Whisk the remaining cream into the custard paste. Pour the custard cream into the egg and sugar mixture. Mix together. Return to the saucepan. Heat gently, stirring continuously, until very thick. Remove the vanilla pod before using.

4 Spoon the warm crème patissiere into the pastry case and spread evenly. Leave to cool before adding the fruit. A layer of cling film placed over the warm crème patissiere will prevent a skin from forming. Brush the finished fruit tart with warm apricot jam.

Thin Pear Pastries

Can be made in advance
Preparation time: *25 minutes*
Cooking time: *30 minutes*

These versatile, elegant pastries will be just as much at home on the afternoon tea table as they will on your dinner party table. You can also use peaches, nectarines or apples.

1   Preheat the oven to 200°C (400°F/gas mark 6).

2   Roast the whole hazelnuts in the oven, for about 10-15 minutes until toasted. Leave to cool.

3   Line a baking tray with baking parchment. Using a 11cm (4½ in) cutter, cut 6 individual rounds from the ready rolled pastry. Place the pastry rounds onto the lined baking tray. Glaze each round with beaten egg yolk.

4   Put the cooled hazelnuts into a food processor and process until ground. Add the marzipan to the ground hazelnuts in the food processor and combine. Add the water drop by drop until a soft paste is formed.

5   Roll out 6 equal balls of the mixture. Place a ball in the centre of each glazed puff pastry round. Flatten the ball with the palm of your hand to fill the centre.

6   Peel, core, quarter and thinly slice the pears.

Serves 6

30g (1oz) skinned hazelnuts
375g (13oz) ready rolled
   puff pastry
2 egg yolks, beaten
100g (4oz) marzipan
1 teasp water
2–3 ripe dessert pears
3 tbs of icing sugar
apricot jam

Position the slices carefully on the marzipan pastry rounds, leaving a 1cm (½ in) pastry border all round. Sieve the icing sugar over the pastries. Bake for approximately 15–20 minutes until golden brown.

7 Remove from the oven and cool. Melt and sieve the apricot jam to make a glaze. Brush each pastry with the glaze.

8 Serve with hazelnut ice cream, Greek yoghurt, cream or ice cream.

Toffee-Apple Crumble

Can be made in advance
Will freeze
Parev option
Preparation time: *15 minutes*
Cooking time: *30 minutes*

In this new twist to an old family favourite, slices of succulent apple bathed in thick gooey toffee custard topped with crunchy crumble – what could be better?

1   Preheat the oven to 180°C (350°/gas mark 4).

2   Make the toffee sauce by heating the butter or margarine, soft brown sugar and golden syrup in a small saucepan. (Before measuring out golden syrup, dip your spoon into very hot water. This prevents the syrup from sticking to the spoon.) Melt completely and boil for 3 minutes until it is golden brown. Remove from the heat and stir in the cream, mixing well.

3   Put all the other ingredients, except for the apples, into a food processor and pulse until they resemble breadcrumbs.

4   Cover the bottom of 8 ramekin dishes or a large ovenproof dish with the prepared apples.

5   Pour the toffee sauce over the sliced apples and mix thoroughly. Cover with the crumble mixture. Bake for 30 minutes.

6   Serve with ice cream or single cream.

Serves 8–10

45g (1½oz) butter or margarine
55g (2oz) dark brown muscavado sugar
6 tbsp golden syrup
250ml (½ pint) double cream (soya cream for a parev option)
75g (2½oz) wholemeal flour
75g (2½oz) plain flour
55g (2oz) rolled oats
75g (2½oz) butter or margarine
75g (2½oz) soft brown sugar
2 tsp cinnamon
2–3 large cooking apples, skinned, cored and finely sliced

To serve
ice cream or single cream

Chocolate Soufflé with a Chocolate and Cointreau Sauce

Can be made in advance
Will freeze
Suitable for Pesach   Parev option
Preparation time: *10 minutes (soufflé); 5 minutes (sauce)*
Cooking time: *10 minutes (soufflé); 5 minutes (sauce)*

Serves 6

50g (2oz) butter or margarine
5 tbs caster sugar, plus extra for
*   dusting*
2 tbs water
100g (3½oz) plain chocolate
6 egg whites
icing sugar
cocoa powder

Sauce
100g (3½oz) plain deluxe
*   chocolate, chopped*
1 tbs Cointreau (for Pesach use
*   a supervised liqueur such as*
*   Sabra)*

1   Preheat the oven to 200°C (400°F/gas mark 6).

2   Put a baking tray, large enough to hold 6 ramekins, into the oven to preheat. Use butter or margarine to grease 6 ramekins then dust with the caster sugar.

3   Make the sugar syrup by melting the caster sugar and water. Boil for about 5 minutes until syrupy.

4   Melt the chocolate in a bowl over a saucepan of simmering water or in the microwave. Add the sugar syrup and mix.

5   Beat the egg whites until they form soft peaks. Add 1 tbs of beaten egg white to the chocolate mixture and fold in using a metal spoon. Fold in the remaining egg whites. Spoon the mixture into the individual ramekins until a quarter full. (You can cover and freeze the soufflés at this stage).

6   Put the ramekins on the pre-heated baking tray. Place in the oven and cook for 10 minutes. (To cook from frozen, add an extra 8–10 minutes to the cooking time.)

7   Make the sauce just before serving. Melt the chocolate until smooth. Add the Cointreau.

8   Dust individual plates with icing sugar and cocoa powder and serve the soufflés as soon as they are ready. Spoon a little of the sauce on top.

Double-Chocolate Baked Alaskas

Can be made in advance
Will freeze
Parev option
Suitable for Pesach
Preparation time: *10 minutes, plus 1 hour 10 minutes freezing time and a further 4 hours final freezing time*
Cooking time : *7 minutes*

Photograph opposite page 172

Serves 8

1 Line a baking tray with baking parchment.

2 Melt the butter or margarine.

3 Place the biscuits and chocolate drops in a food processor and process until they are crumb-like. Stir in the hot, melted butter. Continue processing until combined.

4 Using a 6.5cm (2½ in) round pastry cutter as a template, press the mixture into 8 rounds on the baking sheet. Freeze for 10 minutes.

5 Dip an ice-cream scoop into hot water. Scoop a ball of ice-cream on to each biscuit base. Freeze for for at least 1 hour.

6 Whisk the egg whites, with a pinch of salt, until very stiff. Add the sugar, 1 tbs at a time, whisking after each spoonful. The mixture should be thick and glossy. Spoon or pipe a thick layer of meringue to fully cover the base and ice-cream of each Alaska. Return to the freezer for at least four hours, or overnight.

7 Bake the Alaskas at 220°C (425°F/gas mark 7) for 5–7 minutes until golden. Serve immediately dusted with cocoa powder.

85g (3oz) butter or margarine
225g (8oz) digestive biscuits
  (or Pesach biscuits)
2 tbs plain chocolate drops
570ml (1 pint) chocolate ice
  cream (or use a non-dairy
  equivalent for the parev
  option)
4 egg whites
200g (7oz) caster sugar
pinch of salt
cocoa powder

Lacy Vanilla Apple Pie with Chantilly Cream

Can be made in advance
Will freeze
Parev option
Preparation time: *45 minutes, plus 30 minutes refrigeration for pastry*
Cooking time: *30 minutes*

Serves *6*

300g (10½oz) plain flour
160g (5½oz) cold butter
  or margarine
3 tbs caster sugar, plus extra
  for glazing
1 egg
1 tsp vanilla essence

Filling
4–5 medium sized apples,
  peeled,
  cored and sliced
2 tsp ground cinnamon
zest of 1 large orange, plus the
  juice for glazing
1 tsp plain flour
3 tbs granulated sugar
30g (1oz) cold butter or
  margarine, cut into small
  pieces

Chantilly cream
vanilla pod or vanilla essence
200ml (7fl oz) double cream
100g (4oz) icing sugar

This variation on the traditional apple pie is just as delicious – and will be just as popular.

1　Preheat the oven to 200°C (400°F/gas mark 6).

2　Put the flour and butter in a food processor and mix into breadcrumbs. Pulse in the sugar. Add the egg and vanilla essence and process until the pastry leaves the sides of the bowl.

3　Remove the pastry from the processor, bring together into a ball and flatten with your hands. Wrap in cling film and refrigerate for 30 minutes.

4　Reserve one-third of the pastry for the lacy lid. Roll out the remaining pastry to line a 22cm (9in) deep, loose-bottomed pie dish.

5　Mix the sliced apples with the cinnamon, orange zest, flour and sugar, making sure that you coat the slices thoroughly. Transfer the apple mixture into the prepared bottom pie-crust. Dot with small pieces of the butter.

6　Roll out the reserved pastry into a circle slightly larger than the top of the pie. Cut the rolled pastry circle into 1cm (½in) strips. Arrange half the strips horizontally across the top of the pie, leaving a 1cm (½in) gap between each strip. Repeat this with the remaining strips, arranging them vertically (alternatively you can weave the strips of pastry together). Press the edges together all round the pie to seal.

Non-dairy custard

6 egg yolks
75g (2½oz) caster sugar
500ml (1 pint) soya milk
2 tsp vanilla essence or
* 1 vanilla pod – split*
1 tbs custard powder
1 tbs brandy (optional)

7   Glaze the top with orange juice and a sprinkling of caster sugar. Bake for 30–40 minutes until the pastry is golden brown and the juice in the centre of the pie is bubbling. Leave to cool slightly before serving.

8   Serve with Chantilly Cream, or the non-dairy custard for a parev option.

9   To make the Chantilly cream, split the vanilla pod in half lengthways using scissors and remove the tiny black seeds. Add the seeds or vanilla essence to the cream. Whisk the cream into soft peaks. Add the icing sugar. Continue to whisk until the icing sugar is incorporated.

10 To make the custard, beat the eggs and sugar together until pale and thick. Heat the milk to the boil with the split vanilla pod or essence. Take 1 tbs of the milk and mix with the custard powder to form a paste. Whisk the remaining milk in to the custard paste. Pour the custard milk into the egg and sugar mixture, plus brandy, if using. Mix together. Return to the saucepan. Heat gently, stirring continuously, until the custard coats the back of a spoon. Remove the vanilla pod before serving. The custard can be made up to 4 hours in advance and reheated in the microwave.

Crunchy Nut Biscotti with Red Fruit Compôte

Can be made in advance
Will freeze (biscotti only)
Parev option
Preparation time: *15 minutes, plus 10 minutes cooling time*
Cooking time: *40 minutes*

Makes 60

Biscotti
250g (9oz) plain flour
250g (9oz) caster sugar
½ teasp baking powder
50g (2oz) dried apricots,
*   roughly chopped*
50g (2oz) pitted dates, roughly
*   chopped*
50g (2oz) shelled pistachio nuts
50g (2oz) whole blanched
*   almonds, roughly chopped*
50g (2oz) skinned hazelnuts,
*   roughly chopped*
zest of 1 lemon
2 medium eggs, lightly beaten

Compôte
1 tbs arrowroot
6 tbs fruit liqueur eg cherry
*   brandy*
900g (2lb) mixed berries
*   (including blueberries,*
*   blackcurrants, blackberries,*
*   raspberries, redcurrants, or*
*   900g (2lb) frozen fruits)*

Photograph opposite page 173

These little biscuits go very well with coffee and petit fours, as well as fruit compotes, mousses and soufflés. To ring the changes, serve with a ripe Brie or Camembert as a cheese course, or with crème fraîche.

1   Preheat the oven to 180°C (350°F/gas mark 4).

2   Mix the flour, sugar and baking powder in a large bowl. Add all the dried fruit, nuts and lemon zest. Add three-quarters of the beaten egg and mix well. Add the last quarter a little at a time until the dough takes shape but is not too wet (you may not need all of the egg). If the dough is too sticky, add a little extra flour.

3   Divide the dough into three equal portions. Using your hands, roll each portion into sausage-shapes, about 3cm (1in) in diameter.

4   Place the rolls of dough at least 6cm (2 ½ in) apart on baking trays lined with baking parchment and lightly flatten. Bake until golden brown (for about 20 minutes). Remove from the oven and leave for 10 minutes to cool and firm up.

5   Reduce the temperature of the oven to 140°C (275°F/gas mark 1).

6 Using a serrated knife and cutting diagonally, cut each roll into very thin slices. Lay the slices on the baking trays. Return them to the oven and cook for a further 10 minutes. Turn each biscotti over and cook for another 10 minutes. Remove from the oven. Cool on cake racks. Store the biscotti in airtight containers for up to 2 weeks.

7 To make the compôte, combine the arrowroot, the liqueur and 300ml (½ pint) of cherry juice. Heat in a small saucepan until thickened. Pour the red fruits into the liqueur mixture. Transfer into a glass bowl. Refrigerate until ready to use.

8 Mix the Greek yoghurt and honey together and refrigerate until ready to serve.

9 Serve 3 biscotti with a large spoonful of red fruit compote and some of the honeyed yoghurt.

375g (14oz) 1 tin destoned cherries - drained - keeping the juice

To serve
450g (1lb) Greek yoghurt
4 tbs clear honey

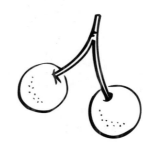

Brandy, Date and Coffee Pudding with Kahlua Zabaglione

Can be made in advance
Will freeze
Parev option
Preparation time: *20 minutes (pudding); 5 minutes (zabaglione)*
Cooking time : *40 minutes (pudding); 15 minutes (zabaglione)*

Serves 8

Pudding
340g (12oz) pitted dates,
*   prunes or sultanas, finely*
*   chopped*
5 tbs strong black coffee
6 tbs brandy
190g (6½oz) soft butter or
*   margarine*
340g (12oz) caster sugar
225g (8oz) plain flour
1 tsp bicarbonate of soda
4 eggs

Zabaglione
6 egg yolks
55g (2oz) caster sugar
2 tbs Kahlua Liqueur
1 tsp instant coffee mixed with
*   2 tbs hot water*

This pudding can be made individually in small pudding bowls or in one large dish. The fruit spiked with the brandy gives this dessert a lively kick, which is enhanced by the complementary Kahlua Zabaglione. This smooth and velvety sauce can accompany many other desserts. Try it with the Thin Pear Pastries (see p.177–178), using a fruit liqueur instead of Kahlua. Zabaglione needs to be made just before it is needed and then used straight away.

1   Lightly grease 8 individual pudding bowls or 1 large bowl.

2   Combine the fruit, coffee and brandy in a small saucepan. Bring to the boil and simmer for 3 minutes. Reserve 3 tbs of the cooking liquid.

3   Drain the fruit and divide equally between the pudding bowls. Cream the butter and sugar together in a large mixing bowl. Beat in the flour, bicarbonate of soda, eggs and reserved cooking liquid and mix well. Pour the pudding mixture over the fruit, filling each pudding bowl until three quarters full.

4   Make 8 foil circles large enough to overlap the top of each bowl by at least 2.5cm (1in) and grease them. Secure a greased foil circle over each bowl with an elastic band.

5   Place the pudding bowls in a single layer in a large

frying pan with a lid. Add enough boiling water to come to two-thirds of the way up the side of the bowls. Bring to the boil and simmer with the lid on for 35 minutes for the individual puddings, or 1½ hours for a large pudding – they are cooked when a skewer is inserted and comes out clean. (At this stage, the puddings can be cooled and frozen. To reheat, defrost for 1 hour at room temperature, cover and put in the oven at 180°C [350°/gas mark] 4 for 30 minutes.)

6 To make the Zabaglione, whisk all the ingredients together in a food mixer. Transfer to a double boiler or to heatproof bowl over a saucepan of simmering water. Whisk vigorously until the mixture has increased to four times its original volume and is pale and fluffy.

7 Invert the puddings or place a slice of one large pudding on to a warm plate. Spoon over some Zabaglione and serve immediately.

Lime Mousse with Almond Biscuits

Can be made in advance
Will freeze
Parev option
Suitable for Pesach
Preparation time: *15 minutes*
Cooking time : *20 minutes*
Cooling time: *30 minutes, plus 4 hours to set*

Serves 8–10

4 tbs water
7g or 1 envelope kosher gelatine
4 eggs, separated
225g (8oz) caster sugar
2 tsp cornflour (or potato flour for Pesach)
zest of 4 limes, and the juice of 3 limes
4 tbs white rum (for Pesach use supervised liqueur), optional
285ml (½ pint) double cream (use whipping cream for a Parev option)
200g (7oz) almond biscuits, crushed (macaroons)

To garnish
2 limes, cut into thin slices

This zingy mousse, with its clean, cool tang, is the ideal finale to a rich meal. It looks particulary impressive when served in balloon wine glasses or brandy balloons. For easy freezing make one large mousse and freeze it in the serving dish.

1 Put the cold water into a medium-sized saucepan. Sprinkle on the gelatine, dissolve over a gentle heat. Do not stir or boil. Then set aside.

2 Combine the egg yolks and sugar in a food mixer. Beat until thick and pale then set aside.

3 Mix 3 tbs of the lime juice with the cornflour. Add the remaining lime juice to the cornflour paste. Combine this well with the cooled gelatine mixture.

4 Combine the egg and lime gelatine mixtures in a deep saucepan and cook over a low heat stirring from time to time until thickened. This will take about 15–20 minutes, taking care not to allow the mixture to boil otherwise it will curdle.

5 Stir 2 tbs of rum, if using, and the reserved lime zest into the pan. Leave the lime custard to cool for about 30 minutes.

6 In a separate bowl whip the double cream until just thick. Gradually whisk the remaining rum, if using,

into the cream. Using a metal spoon, fold the cream
into the cooled lime custard.

7 In a separate bowl beat the egg whites until stiff
peaks are formed. Fold 1 tbs of egg white into the
lime mixture using a metal spoon, to loosen the
mixture. Fold in the rest of the egg whites in the
same way.

8 Spoon 3 tbs of mousse into each wine glass. Sprinkle
over 2 tbs of the crushed biscuits. Divide the
remaining mousse equally between the glasses. Top
with the rest of the biscuits. Leave to set for a
minimum of 4 hours or overnight in the fridge.

9 Serve garnished with slices of freshly cut lime.

Cinnamon Bread with Hot Cherries and Ice Cream

Can be made in advance
Parev
Preparation time: *10 minutes*
Cooking time: *5 minutes*

Serves *6*

1 tbs arrowroot
2 tins cherries, stoned
*300ml (½ pint) juice saved
 from the tins of cherries*
*2 tbs crème de cassis or
 kiddush wine*
*6 thick slices of cinnamon
 bread, or brioche, or challah*
icing sugar
cinnamon
*570ml (1 pint) ice cream of
 your choice*

This is a hot, amazingly quick dessert that everyone will enjoy. It can be made with store cupboard ingredients so it is perfect for when you have unexpected guests. Mascarpone cheese or fromage frais make interesting alternatives to the ice-cream.

1 Mix the arrowroot with 2 tbs of cherry juice to form a thin paste. Add the rest of the juice and crème de cassis. Heat in a saucepan over a medium heat until thickened stirring continuously. Add the cherries to the syrup – this can be made in advance and heated when required.

2 Dust the bread with icing sugar and cinnamon, then toast or grill.

3 Cut the toast in half and place one half on a warmed plate. Pour over 2 tbs of hot cherries. Place the other slice of bread on top at an jaunty angle. Add one more tablespoon of cherries. Dust the plate with cinnamon and icing sugar.

4 Serve immediately with ice cream (parev for a meat meal).

Parev Hazelnut Ice Cream

Can be made in advance
Will freeze
Pesach friendly
Preparation time: *30 minutes*
Cooking time: *20 minutes; plus 15 minutes cooling praline;*
30 minutes cooling the custard; 4 hours freezing

Photograph opposite page 173

This partners thin pear pastries, plum and apricot tatin, toffee apple crumble and lacy vanilla apple pie brilliantly.

To make the Praline

1 Pre-heat the oven to 200°C (400°F/gas mark 6).

2 Line a baking tray with baking parchment. Spread the hazelnuts in a single layer on the tray. Toast them in the oven for 10–15 minutes until golden brown – be careful not to burn.

3 Remove from the oven and set aside.

4 Dissolve the sugar and water in a heavy-based saucepan over a medium heat and continue to cook until a rich golden caramel is formed.

5 Immediately pour the caramel over the roasted hazelnuts. Leave to cool.

6 When this is cold and set, transfer to a food processor and pulse into small pieces. (This can be made upto 1 week in advance and stored in an airtight container).

Serves 8-10

Praline
250g (9oz) skinned hazelnuts
225g (8oz) caster sugar
3 tbs water

Parev hazelnut
ice cream
500ml (1 pint) soya cream
750ml (1 pint) sweetened soya
  milk
7 egg yolks
175g (6oz) caster sugar
2 tbs cornflour (or potato
  flour for Pesach)

To make the ice cream

1 Combine the soya cream and soya milk in a large saucepan. Heat until just below boiling point. Remove from heat.

2 Whisk the egg yolks and sugar together until pale and thick. Add the cornflour to the egg mixture and whisk together briefly.

3 Pour the warmed milk mixture onto the egg mixture and whisk together.

4 Return to the heat and continue to cook over a low heat — stirring constantly to prevent curdling (do not boil).

5 When the mixture is thick enough to coat the back of a wooden spoon, Remove from the heat and pour in to a bowl. Leave to cool for ½ hour.

6 Mix the hazelnut crumbs into the custard base and freeze in a suitable container for a minimum of 4 hours. Remove from the freezer about 30 minutes before serving or microwave carefully until softened.

Index of Recipes and Ingredients

Index of Parev and Festival Recipes